Libraries in the Age of Mediocrity

With Best
Wishes

[signature]

LIBRARIES IN THE AGE OF MEDIOCRITY

by
EARL LEE

(Author of *Drakulya*)

McFarland & Company, Inc., Publishers
Jefferson, North Carolina and London

British Library Cataloguing-in-Publication data are available

Library of Congress Cataloguing-in-Publication Data

Lee, Earl, 1954–
    Libraries in the age of mediocrity / by Earl Lee.
       p. cm.
    Includes index.
    ISBN 0-7864-0548-1 (sewn softcover : 55# alkaline paper) ∞
    1. Library science — United States.   I. Title.
  Z665.2.U6L44   1998
  020'.973 — dc21   98-24669
                                            CIP

Manufactured in the United States of America

McFarland & Company, Inc., Publishers
  Box 611, Jefferson, North Carolina 28640

For Kathy

Contents

Preface

The essays in this book are all previously unpublished, with the exception of "A Visit to Oz," which is based on two articles that appeared in *Librarians at Liberty*. This book may be characterized as either "libertarian" or "postmodern" although I am not personally wedded to either term. Certainly, the essay "Libraries, Libertarianism and the State" can be said to show how libertarianism was used by A. Broadfield as a foundation for a philosophy of librarianship and how this approach can still be used today. Certainly, historically, libertarianism has been a pillar of librarianship, including a wide variety of views to the Left and Right of A. Broadfield's, from the libertarian socialism of Ervin Szabo to the libertarian capitalism of Ben Franklin.

The following three chapters, "Censorship and Community Standards," "Library Automation in the Age of Mediocrity" and "The Postmodern Library," explore the dilemmas of modern library practice as we move from the modern into the postmodern age. It is my purpose to use the techniques of postmodernism to examine and deconstruct both libraries, as modernist institutions, and our society at large. The chapter "Target ALA" and those following should be read as examples of how this social critique can be carried forward.

I want to thank Robert Walter, Dean of Learning Resources at Leonard H. Axe Library, Pittsburg State University, for allowing me the time and resources to complete this manuscript. I would also like to thank Sanford Berman and Charles Willett for their encouragement over the last few years. But especially I want to thank my wife Kathy for her special editorial skills, for pointing out at least some of my half-baked or hare-brained ideas (I left those in the book) and for giving me the chance to rethink some of my prejudices.

I also want to thank my parents — my mother for my Irish temper and my father for that German stubbornness and the "touch of dark blood" that make the whole mongrel mess seem to work together somehow.

Chapter 1

A Visit to Oz; or, "Pay No Attention to the Man Behind the Curtain!": Case Studies in the Political Economy of Library Automation

I

A few years ago during the Kansas Library Association convention, I went with a group of twenty or so librarians on a tour of the local university library. As the group of librarians wound its way through the large Cataloging workroom, someone asked our tour guide what kind of backlog they had. The guide smiled politely as she said, "Our backlog is not significant."

Not particularly satisfied with this answer, another librarian persisted in wanting to know how large the backlog was. Our guide, positively beaming, responded, "About six months."

Later, the tour went into the public area and passed the old card catalog and the terminals for the new online catalog. Our guide began to praise the quality of their new online system and said that the library was developing plans to get rid of the old card catalog by the end of the year. At this point someone (probably the same someone mentioned earlier) asked our guide if all the library's older book holdings were already listed in the new computer system. The guide smiled as she said, "Most of our books are in the system. The part of our collection not in the system will be added later in a retro project. It is not a significant part of the collection."

At this point a little alarm bell went off in my head. Someone dared to press on, "How much of your collection is not in the new computer system?"

Our guide smiled, beaming with confidence, "Only about 40 percent of the collection." Several of the librarians on the tour nodded in wonder and awe as witnesses to the amazing miracle of automation. And a few of us stared at our shoes, not daring to look each other in the eye, and felt a common shudder at the strange new world of the information age.

As a librarian who has worked with several library systems, including the traditional system based on 3×5 paper cards, a microcomputer-based acquisitions system, and a few mainframe-based systems, I feel I came to our library's automation project with a fairly good sense of what computers can and can't do, when compared with the old card catalogs. Nothing, however, prepared me for the reality I found.

Most library directors and library staffs, as they approach the purchase of an automated system, share many assumptions about what an automated library system should do — assumptions that are simply not true. This is part of our common culture and training as librarians. We believe that a library system must obviously perform certain basic functions, like producing intelligible statistics. In fact, library automation vendors have a quite different vision of what is important and what is "not significant."

Many professional librarians enjoy a good deal of autonomy in their jobs. Most patrons want the job done right and don't really care about the nuts-and-bolts of how we do it. This autonomy effectively ends with automation, both in controlling how the system works and even in selecting which system to buy. Acquiring an automated system means giving up most of your control over bibliographic access to your collection.

First of all, most librarians think that when the time comes to decide which automated system they will buy, they will have the final say on which computer system they get. In fact, the decision will most likely be made by someone outside the library. In general, the more expensive the library system, the more likely the decision will be made by someone else.

Case 1: The librarians at a small state university library in Kansas were making plans to automate. They investigated their options and decided which features were important. They knew what they wanted their new computer system to do for them. They asked for proposals (RFPs), evaluated the proposals from the vendors, and prepared to negotiate with the vendors. In addition to the vendors' reps, present at the negotiations were the library director, the university's MIS officer, and a representative of the state agency which approves all computer purchases in Kansas.

As the negotiations progressed, it became clear to everyone present that the library favored getting a Unisys-based system. And then came the surprise. At this point, suddenly the state agency, which has veto power over computer purchases, decided to withdraw permission for the negotiations to continue. Up until now, all the other state universities who had purchased computer systems had taken the IBM-based system which appeared to be "favored" by the agency.

The negotiations were over. At this point everyone went home to try to decide what to do next. Clearly the university would need a lot of political muscle if it planned to go against the agency's decision. In looking into the problem, the librarians discovered that a year earlier the state treasurer's office had gone into battle with this same agency over buying a Unisys computer. It is rumored that, at one point in the "discussion," the agency representative became angry that the treasurer was stubbornly refusing to buy the computer brand he recommended, and he became verbally abusive with her. However, she resisted his verbal attacks and was able to bring enough political pressure to bear, eventually getting her own way and buying the mainframe she wanted, in spite of his agency's opposition. The fact that the state treasurer, with all the political pull she could muster, just barely managed to get her own way did not bode well.

A few days later, after discussions with the university administration, it became clear that no one in the administration really wanted to go to the mat on this issue; the prudent decision would be to take the IBM-based system, or face the possibility of not getting a system at all.

At this point, fate took a hand. A month after the library was refused permission to buy a system, the state treasurer, who had become a dark-horse candidate for governor, defeated a former governor of Kansas to become the Democratic nominee. In November, she went on to defeat the incumbent and became Kansas' first woman governor.

Suddenly, the state agency which had earlier opposed the university purchasing a non–IBM system became very conciliatory and suggested that the university buy whatever system the librarians wanted.

However, rather than buy the Unisys-based system that the librarians wanted, the campus administration had a better idea. The university's MIS officer decided that the library should buy a PRIME-based system or let him develop his own home-grown system, which would, of course, also be run on a PRIME computer. Needless to say, the library bought a PRIME-based system. Several years later, after PRIME stopped making computers, the library began making plans to migrate to another computer system, which would be an IBM-based system. Such is the karma of automation.

The point here is that at no time was the library's opinion or possible objections considered of any compelling importance to the final decision. The outcome of the state elections had more influence on the final decision than the librarians did. This is probably also the case in most automation decisions, as virtually all libraries seem to follow the line of least resistance in their "choice" of automated systems.

> *Principle 1:* Libraries "choose" to purchase the system that runs on the local computer box favored by the MIS people, unless the MIS officer is overruled by higher-ups in the administration or the city, county, or state governments.

*   *   *

Even more bizarre than the selection of a computer system is what happens during and after the contract between the vendor and the library is signed.

Case 2: In the RFP (request for proposal) submitted to the vendors and in the contract signed with the vendor, a college library required an Interlibrary Loan module and a number of special features, including the ability to create a "new books" list that could be circulated to the faculty.

In fact, when the system was brought up, the Interlibrary Loan "module" was discovered to be a series of work-around procedures, essentially driven off the Circulation module. The need to support the interlibrary loan function continues to this day to be a sore point with the Circulation department. Furthermore, the "special" Reserve Room module has never worked right; and the so-called "New Books" list was little more than a list of all the authors and titles of books ordered, even those that had not yet been received or cataloged, and in no particular order. In fact, the required special features that were promised in the contract were there as part of the system, but these features didn't work the way they should have and didn't meet the minimum standards that any rational person would accept.

Principle 2: The features described in the contract may, by some strange accident, bear a vague resemblance to the functions actually delivered by the vendor.

*   *   *

The political economy of library automation probably most clearly resembles the way the Pentagon works with the large corporations it does business with. The relationship, despite what you would logically expect, clearly gives complete control of the relationship to the vendors and the process is so inefficient, so flawed, and so one-sided that you wonder why the United States has not yet been conquered by Cuba. Except, of course, the Cuban procurement system is even more politically loaded than ours.

Case 3: The librarians at a medium-sized library, after signing a contract with a vendor and going through installation and training, were very dissatisfied with the system they had acquired. They made a series of complaints — pointing out how the system failed to work properly — and sent dozens of letters and faxes to the vendor documenting the failures, and they even made not-so-vague threats that they would not accept the system and sign off on the various modules, until they were fixed.

The vendor's only response was to show the librarians several awkward and tedious work-arounds (actually developed by other libraries) and to suggest that, once the library accepted the system by signing off on the modules, they could move from the Install Team (made up of overworked wet-behind-the-ears computer hackers) to the Regular Support Team (made up of kind and saintly gurus of automation). The library resisted this tack, which would have been a kind of capitulation, and continued to send faxes (and copies of faxes, as the originals tended to get "lost" by the Install Team).

After several months of complaints and trying to deal with the inept hacking of the Install Team, the library finally gave up, signed off on the system, and were delivered from the rough-handling of the Install Team to the more subtle purgatory of the Regular Support Team. The librarians had come to look on the Install Team as a group of little boys who, as children, must have spent their time spraying anthills with a fire hose; they were delighted with the tender mercies of the new Support Team, who — based on their current behavior — must have used only squirt guns.

> *Principle 3:* The power relationship between the vendor and the library is very one-sided. The library has virtually no power to force changes from the vendor, and the library depends on the good will of the vendor to get even minimal help in dealing with the system.

*   *   *

Many librarians, in reading about library automation, wonder at all the wonderful adjectives used by library directors to describe the automated system they bought. They are especially surprised by these "glowing" reports, if they actually work on a day-to-day basis with one of these wonderful systems. And, secretly, many librarians suspect the glowing reports to be the product of mental illness.

Case 4: A cataloger in a large public library in Ohio, frustrated with months of trying to deal with the peculiar workings of his new cataloging module, went to the library director to complain (again) about lack of response from the vendor. In fact, when indexes were being built, the catalogers were locked out of the system for days, or even weeks. Tape loads of new software releases also tied up the system, when the system wasn't crashing on its own in the middle of the night. The library assistants were all on the verge of a collective nervous breakdown, and one was doing research in his spare time to discover how to properly tie a hangman's noose.

The director, who in the past had been generally sympathetic to the cataloger's problems, was defensive. This was the same director who had, last year, criticized the cataloger about a one-month delay in processing standing orders through cataloging. Now, a two-month delay in getting the standing orders through acquisitions, caused by new software, did not seem to bother him. Instead, his suggestion was, "Put them through using the old paper 3 × 5 slips and do the work on the system later."

Principle 4: The choice of a library system, like any choice involving the personal judgment and prestige of your boss, is not to be criticized to the person responsible for the original decision — at least not if you value your own job.

*   *   *

Given the fact of having purchased a system, most librarians think that the vendor, desiring their continuing goodwill, will be responsive to their problems and quick to make good on their mistakes. In fact, while this may be true for your local grocer, it doesn't apply to your vendor.

Case 5: A Systems librarian, after years of struggling with a Reserve module that didn't work very well and a Circulation module whose reports were often wrong, when they were even intelligible, decided to volunteer her library to be a beta test site for a new software release. She felt that, if nothing else, she would at least get them to fix the Reserve module.

The vendor promised three to four programmers would visit the site when the software was loaded and that support for the beta test sites would exceed her wildest dreams. Surely, she thought, this is the land of milk and honey promised by her library school professors in days of yore.

In fact, the three programmers arrived on Friday and left on Sunday with the system not exactly working right. The Systems librarian had agreed to use "ghost" indexes until the new indexes could be built with the new software, but in fact the new indexes were not working right either. When she contacted the other test sites, she discovered that all the other libraries, unable to build the new indexes, were still using "ghost" indexes after several months. At one of the test sites, the Systems librarian discovered, in trying to build the new subject index, that the index was, in fact, indexing every word in the MARC record, not just the subjects — and was only halfway through the job after running for two weeks.

The Systems librarian frantically called the other sites to ask for help and suggestions. Undaunted by the problems, the vendor continued to promise its other clients that the new software release would be available "later this month" and did not see the lack of working indexes as a hindrance to the distribution of the new release.

To further complicate the issue, the vendor, while working with the data files, accidentally deleted all the cursive *l*'s from the call numbers in the library's MARC records. In an act of contrition, the vendor apologized profusely and gave the Systems librarian a list of the records that had been affected, while strongly suggesting that the library stop using cursive *l*'s in their call numbers.

Adding insult to injury, several months later the vendor came up with a "fix" for the problem with the cursive 1's. The automated system now has a software feature that automatically changes cursive 1's into roman 1's for all OCLC records that are downloaded into the system. Actually fixing the system so that it would accommodate cursive 1's never appeared to be an option.

> *Principle 5:* A library vendor is not quite as reliable as a good used car salesman. At least with the used car salesman you can go somewhere else next time. With a vendor, your best quality is that latent streak of masochism that almost all systems librarians seem to develop on the job.

*   *   *

In fact, an automation vendor is only willing to do the bare minimum necessary to keep his current clients happy. His real interest is in putting up a good front and getting as many new clients as possible — even if the vendor can't possibly serve these new clients with anything like a bare minimum of support. The main interest of the vendor is in profit, which means *growth* and developing a range of new products, new services, and new software releases to attract new business. Developing a solid, consistent product that actually does what the librarians expect it to do — at present this is a utopian fantasy.

Case 6: The Automation librarian dutifully went through the task of filling out forms and "organizing" (i.e., prodding) the rest of the staff to fill out forms describing exactly which fields they wanted indexed when the new software release was installed. After several weeks of carefully laying out the mapping of the indexes, based on OCLC MARC format, they mailed the forms to the vendor.

Several weeks passed. The Automation librarian called the vendor several times to check on how the process was going, but the vendor never bothered to return his calls. Finally, the day before the software was to be installed, he got a call from the vendor at 4:45 P.M. to give him a rundown of what was going on. As the Automation librarian shuffled through the stack of forms and tried to run down an OCLC manual, the vendor "described" (i.e., decided) what fields the system was going to use and how it was to be mapped, essentially ignoring the forms submitted by the library staff.

After the phone call, the Automation librarian recalled that much the same thing had happened with earlier forms sent out by the vendor. The software was not customized to the extent that the forms suggested, leading him to suspect that the whole process of submitting forms was only a ruse by the vendor to "lead on" potential customers. Automation vendors are all too familiar with the old "bait and switch" game.

Later, when the documentation for the new software release was sent out, the Automation librarian discovered that a function available on the current release was not available in the newer version. The ability to go to certain screens and change data was vital to one of the work-arounds given him by another library. When he called to ask that the vendor continue to give them the authority to go to these screens, the vendor gave him a flat "No." When he pressed the issue, explaining how important is was to libraries to be able to have this function in order to do their day-to-day processing, he was told point-blank, "That function is not part of the philosophy of the new release."

> *Principle 6:* A Ford dealer is reported to have said, when the company first began production on the Model T, "People can have any color car they want, as long as it is black"; seventy-five years later this basic principle still applies, even in areas like automation where, theoretically, customization of the product for each consumer should be relatively easy.
>
> *   *   *

Where many other areas of the business world have, for the last decade, worked hard at developing quality control and customer service, these concepts are still apparently quite alien to library automation vendors. Anyone who buys an automated system expecting quality or service is sadly deluding himself as to the reality of the modern automated library.

II

"They did it to me; they can do it to you." This line from the film *The Net* didn't really scare me much. Having worked with automated library systems for some years now, I'm pretty much convinced that the computer villains of the real world are too incompetent to threaten us with more than minor inconveniences. Not only that, they are scared of what their critics say about them in the *print* media, showing us that the printed word, combined with radio and television, is still the main molder of public opinion. The inflated info-tech-chat about the "Web" is still just big talk from a bunch of teenage boys, mostly trying to show each other who has the biggest disk drive.

Even when America Online decided to electronically bill my checking account for a month of service I hadn't requested, all I had to do was pick up the telephone (a technology now close to a century old) and call my credit union to tell them to refuse America Online's electronic draft. Case closed. America Online is still trying to entice my teenage son to use AOL again, but he knows that his old dad will make him pay for the long-distance calls out of his allowance. Again, case closed.

The major hullabaloo generated over "Windows 95" is, however, a different story. Here is a masterpiece of marketing. A chorus of media gurus has gotten together and sold America, and the world, a mediocre piece of software that is a poor imitation of Apple Computer's operating system. Worse yet, they have convinced computer systems designers that everything has to run on Windows 95, or failing that, it needs to at least *look* like Windows. Unfortunately, the systems designers who work on the automated library system I use have joined this crowd of intellectual pygmies, falling on their knees to worship at the altar of Bill "The Great and Powerful" Gates.

Granted that I wasn't particularly happy with my old acquisitions system. It was awkward, stubborn, and, like all automated systems, full of more than its share of bugs and quirks. Compared with the ETTACQ system I used years ago, it was as maneuverable as a dinosaur. For several years in the late 1980s, I ran library acquisitions off of ETTACQ, a micro-based system that cost less than a thousand dollars. It kept track of orders, vendor statistics, and funds. Then the university bought an integrated library system that runs on the university mainframe and costs hundreds of thousands of dollars. Unfortunately, the new system couldn't keep track of vendor discounts, and trying to cancel an order was like engaging in hand-to-hand combat with a "Street Fighter" video game.

The new software release for this system is even worse. It makes me yearn for the days when we ran everything with 3×5 slips of paper. The new software release has fake "Windows"-looking screens, but it is now twice as hard to use. With the old system, you could simply hit the <Enter> key to go past the fields you didn't want to change, moving through fields in consecutive order, linearly down the page. With the new system you have to arrow around the screen looking for the fields you have to change. I'd guess this new system should cut speed and efficiency by about 30 percent.

For some time I mulled over this question: Why is it that a micro-based acquisitions system running off an old IBM-clone 286 machine can work more efficiently than a mainframe system developed by an army of systems designers and programmers? This question puzzled me for years. And then last week I went down to the drugstore and tried to buy a tube of Whitfield's Ointment.

For those of you who haven't heard of Whitfield's Ointment, I should mention that it is the only cure for athlete's foot known to humankind — and thereby hangs the tale. In the mid–1970s I lived in a college dorm and picked up a bad case of athlete's foot in one of the dormitory showers. I tried a dozen different ointments and powders, but they did little more than slow the spread. It turned into a World War I–style battle of trench warfare, lasting more than three years. Then one day I mentioned my problem to a law school student and he told me to buy some Whitfield's Ointment. I was surprised by how cheap it was, as you can buy a tube for less than $2, whereas most other ointments run $5 to $7 a tube.

If you go into a drug store today, it is impossible to find Whitfield's Ointment. The stores often have several shelves devoted to almost useless powders and salves that do little more than give relief for the itching. The question then is, since Whitfield's Ointment actually cures athlete's foot, why is it that you can't find it on the shelves? The answer, in one word, is marketing.

The formula for Whitfield's Ointment is an old one, and it is no longer controlled by a particular drug company. Anyone can make it, and so no one has a vested interest in promoting it. The other newer athlete's foot preparations have newer formulas that are patented and controlled by individual drug companies. These drug companies have a vested interest in promoting and marketing *their* product. And the last thing they want is to compete with an ointment that actually cures athlete's foot. And they have the economic clout to force drugstores *not* to carry Whitfield's Ointment.

In a sense, this is a variation on the whole debate about "planned obsolescence." Like the companies that make cars that fall apart after ten years, or tools that wear out after eight years, or appliances whose works seize up after seven years, the drug companies have to think in terms of making a product that relieves most of the symptoms of an ailment, but *without* actually curing it. After all, if a person can cure his athlete's foot with a one-time purchase of a $2 tube of ointment, who is going to buy salves costing $5 or $7 that only give temporary relief? And this is where marketing comes in.

Postmodern corporations have discovered that it is easier and more cost-effective to make claims through advertisements, rather than actually try to make a good product. A phone company can spend more money on advertising than the GNP of Finland, convincing us that we want to be able to receive faxes while standing on the beach, instead of giving us cheap, reliable long-distance service. It is easier to manipulate consumers through advertising than to try to compete on a level playing field with other companies. The last thing a postmodern corporation would want to do is actually expose itself to the market forces of supply and demand. The last thing these companies need is for consumers to realize that "The Great and Powerful Oz" is really a seedy con-artist, palming off a designer watch in place of a heart, a diploma in place of real knowledge, and a military medal in place of courage. The marketing hucksters don't want a fair comparison of their product with other products. What would happen to their sales figures if we discover, as Dorothy did in *The Wizard of Oz*, that we can get a pair of good walking shoes for far less than the price of an over-inflated hot-air balloon whose direction you can't even control?

For this reason, drug companies want to convince us that we are getting relief for our ailments, combining high-powered marketing with a placebo effect. This is more clever and profitable than producing a product that really *cures* what ails us. That would be like killing the goose that lays the golden eggs. Providing temporary relief of symptoms is much more profitable in the long run. Similarly, our automated library system is not just a one-time purchase. We have to pour tens of thousands of dollars into it each year for upgrades, maintenance agreements, etc., etc., etc. My old micro-based system was a sneeze in a handkerchief compared to the tornado of costs associated with current mainframe-based systems. And every time we get a new software release, we get a whole new batch of bugs that need to be fixed, patches on poor designs, etc., etc., etc., in a continuing cycle. And there is no end in sight.

The older software for our mainframe system was a pain to deal with, but you could make it work, sort of. And the company seemed happy enough to sell it to us and to everyone else in sight. The problem was that, when the company's salesmen went to library conventions, some librarians would look at their product and say, "It doesn't *look* like the other library systems." Many of the other library systems had already gone to that fake "Windows"-looking computer display. And so every time sales took a slump, the salesmen would complain to their bosses, "The librarians say it doesn't *look* like the other 'Windows' systems." And then they would say, "We could really sell a lot of these systems if they looked more like the other library systems." And then the bosses go to the software developers and say, "Make the system look like a 'Windows' product; the librarians hate library systems that don't look like other library systems."

Unfortunately, in the marketing-driven postmodern corporation the offhand comments parroted by salesmen carry a lot more weight than advice coming from the librarians who actually work with the system. Most automation vendors have a network, either formal or informal, of librarians who work with their products and give them plenty of good advice on how to make their products work better. But most companies are more concerned with marketing — meaning getting new customers — than with keeping their current customers happy. And so marketing wins over product development every day. So someday we may have a library system that receives faxes on the beach, but it probably won't have a decent interface between the Serials module and the Acquisitions module, let alone a functional ILL module. That idea is still far, far away. Somewhere over the rainbow.

III

Recently, one of the largest automation vendors in the country went through a major change, including completely redesigning its Acquisitions module. Many of the librarians who use this module on a day-to-day basis have, over the years, complained, sent letters, faxes and e-mail, formed committees — all giving helpful suggestions as to how the system could be improved. None of this, of course, made much difference to the vendor — after all, the vendor already had these chumps "on the hook."

The changes and redesign of the Acquisitions module came about because a potential customer — a national library with a large number of affiliated libraries — demanded that the vendor upgrade its Acquisitions module before the librarians would even consider buying this automated system for their libraries.

The vendor — positively drooling over "The Big Sale" — decided to spend the money to redesign the system, looking particularly at the Acquisitions module. The main complaint of the national library was that the automated system did not handle Standing Orders very well. This was, of course, only one of several features that desperately needed to be fixed, but it was the particular obstacle to selling the librarians the automated library system.

After six months, the vendor came up with a completely redesigned system. Then the vendor set up classes to train its old customers on how to use the new system, and quickly began issuing newly revised versions of the software to all its current library customers. The classes were a two-day session that introduced librarians to the new features, so that they would understand the fundamentals of how the new software worked.

These training classes covered just the bare minimum, which means that they did not cover how to process Standing Orders or Gifts at all. Meanwhile, the new manuals printed by the vendor and sent out to all the library customers did not mention Standing Orders or Gifts (and neither term appears in the index to the new manual). Only after the new module had been in place for several months did the software designers come up with a procedure for handling Gifts and Standing Orders. It was clearly one of their "on the fly" work-around procedures, probably developed by one of the librarians at one of the beta test sites.

By this time, the big national library was already on board as a customer, having made the contractual commitment to buy this system. And so, of course, the vendor quickly lost interest in making the Acquisitions module work any better than it already did. Today, more than two years after the release of the new software, the process for receiving Standing Orders still doesn't work properly. Much like the so-called Interlibrary

Loan system (which actually runs off the Circulation module), Standing Orders are processed as if they were a subset or a variation on the regular Firm Orders. Essentially, in order to receive a Standing Order, the librarian simply duplicates an old Standing Order. It is a bit inconvenient, as every time you dupe an order the system forces you to print it (but, hey, it's just paper!).

Oddly enough, once a Standing Order is received, the system shows it as "Closed" (which would be o.k. for a Firm Order). Librarians, who by now are pretty jaded and used to doing work-arounds, did not bother to notify the vendor that standing orders were showing as "Closed" in the system, and so several years passed before the problem was recorded as a "bug." Needless to say, the programmers will stay up nights working on this problem, and they will probably come up with a "patch" that will make the process of receiving Standing Orders even more inconvenient than it already is.

It is unlikely that the vendor will ever get around to creating a separate module/process that deals with Standing Orders. Once the vendor had the big new customer "on the hook," further work on the new Acquisitions module was limited to the regular "upgrades" of the software and fixes of the always-present "bugs" and "glitches" in the software.

Most people, unfamiliar with automated systems, would be shocked to see how many "bugs" and "fixes" there are. In a typical month, the number of bugs, just in Acquisitions, runs to well over a dozen. These bugs are, of course, mostly discovered by librarians using the system. And, of course, some fixes are actually "custom designs" that someone else paid to get, and that you will have to pay for too, if you want that particular function in your library. It's enough to make your feet itch!

Just out of curiosity, I recently went to the internet and tried to find out if anyone out there still sells Whitfield's Ointment—the only product known to humankind that actually cures athlete's foot. Oddly enough, I found the product listed in a Hong Kong government formulary as one of many cheap, effective products that work quite well for common ailments (of poor people). The only criticism it had of Whitfield's Ointment was that it is "cheap and effective but cosmetically less acceptable than the modern proprietary antifungals." The word "proprietary" means that he, like most doctors, thinks you should really buy only those drugs patented and controlled by large pharmaceutical companies.

The doctor's critical comment "cosmetically less acceptable" struck me as rather odd. After all, who cares what the bottom of your feet look like "cosmetically"? And if you are out walking around on the beach (wearing sandals, one hopes), wouldn't it look better to have your feet *cured* of athlete's foot, rather than still being covered with blisters, pustules and infection? This is the kind of double-talk you get from doctors, who depend on pharmaceutical companies for much of their income (after all, if you could buy something over-the-counter to cure what ails you, and without a prescription, you wouldn't need to see the doctor). The whole doctor/pharmacy relationship is an efficient system for extorting money out of sick people. This is proven conclusively by the fact that so many drugs, once the patent runs out, are then sold over the counter. If the purpose of writing prescriptions is to protect the public from dangerous drugs, then how can a prescription drug become an over-the-counter drug? (I guess you can tell that I'm determined to get cheap drugs!)

Needless to say, this doctor's concern for "cosmetic" appearances harkens back to the obsession of salesmen to have a "Windows-looking" automated system. Again, it doesn't matter how lousy the system works, as long as it looks like a Windows-based system. A system that works better but isn't glitzy enough, that would be a *bad* thing, in the view of most salesmen.

Currently, OCLC Inc., probably the largest vendor of computer services in the world, is busily working to get all its products functioning in a "Windows" version. Like the rest of the automation vendors, OCLC is being dragged down the garden path in trying to follow the latest "trend." OCLC has a reputation for bringing out new products long after everyone else, much like IBM, and then trying to capture the market. Luckily, OCLC has proved itself over and over again to be very good at delivering basic services, while less than efficient in creating glitzy new "products." Unfortunately, like Dynix, Notis, and the rest of the automation vendors, systems people at OCLC are obsessed with trying to *look* up-to-date, and they seem to take this "Windows" junk very seriously.

In fact, we will never really understand the thinking of library automation vendors, or book vendors, or even publishers for that matter, until we understand the mentality of the postmodern corporation. To the postmodern corporation, appearances are far more important than reality. Only a postmodern corporation would — as one company did recently — donate $1,000 to a young boy who needed a new wheelchair and then spend $100,000 on advertising to brag about how generous the company was to give him the money for his wheelchair. The fact that a corporate manager or executive does not see this behavior as a problem is, itself, an indication of just how bad things have gotten.

The library automation industry has a long way to go before it becomes as efficient (i.e., ethically challenged) as the medical/pharmaceutical industry in this country. For example, the medical community has for many years promoted vasectomy as a safe procedure without any side effects. In truth, vasectomy does have side effects, but they are not studied by medical researchers. Why, you might ask, don't they study this? The answer is simple. Surgeons earn a *lot* of money every year performing vasectomies. They earn a lot of money, too, in performing surgery to reverse vasectomies. And so no one in the medical profession has any interest in documenting the "side effects" of vasectomy. Similarly, the insurance companies save enormous amounts of money each year as the result of the lower number of pregnancies and births, so they don't want to hear about side effects either. They all make money off this surgical procedure, and so none of them want to rock the boat. Understanding this may help you to understand why so many librarians complain bitterly about their crummy automated library systems, at least among themselves, but you never hear about it in the professional journals. Just look in these journals and see who buys advertising. None of the popular library publications are going to touch this issue, because it's not in their financial interest to do so. Similarly, no one is going to make friends or influence people by criticizing library automation. It is the sacred cow of our profession; and it almost always takes someone outside the profession, like novelist Nicholson Baker or author Clifford Stoll, to raise these issues.

But the biggest fraud perpetrated by the people who promote automation, whether it is library automation or automation in other fields, is the idea that automation is a labor-saving improvement. In fact, since our library automated, I've had to take over handling the creation of all our firm orders and the receiving of all our orders, including the standing orders. These were tasks that were once handled by students, but now I have to do it, because our order system is so complex and inflexible that I can't afford to have any mistakes made in the way materials are ordered and received. Furthermore, we have the Systems librarian constantly breathing down our necks with printouts of problems that need to be corrected. The classified staff are even more enchanted than I am by these "labor-saving improvements." Every time the Systems librarian enters the back room carrying a printout, they begin muttering to themselves and looking for a closet to hide in.

Once you get an automated system, the day will come when the Systems librarian will walk into your office, carrying a printout of several hundred (or, if you're particularly unlucky, several thousand) records that were "accidentally" corrupted with the global-change command. The Systems librarian will put the printout on your desk, apologize for the mistake, and suggest that you need to manually correct these records as soon as possible. That day will come. If you're very lucky, it will only happen to you once or twice (in the first year).

Also, the advent of your new computerized catalog will mark the beginning of what is called "clean-up" of your database. You might think that this can be accomplished in a year or two. In fact, we are still hard at it five years later, and there is no end in sight. In most cases, the energy you once expended in filing catalog cards will now be expended in data clean-up. You might as well plan for this now.

Finally, if you are particularly unlucky, the library director will decide to make your library part of a consortium of several libraries, all sharing the same automated system. Some automated systems handle this better than others, but no matter which system you have, expect *big* headaches and constant battles with your wonderful consortium "partners." At the same time, you might feel a little sorry for your new partners, as they are coming into this project with the same delusions about automated systems that you once had.

In the 15th century, a brutal and vicious Transylvanian prince could get his jollies by impaling hundreds of people right and left — and if he were particularly angry, he would use a blunted stake. Later, in the 18th century, a French marquis could enjoy the more refined pleasures of whipping hired ladies, or perhaps burning them with melted candle wax (a trick Madonna uses in one of her more recent movies). Most of us would call this progress (I think?). But today, with the power and sophistication of computers, it is possible to torture people in more subtle ways.

If you, like the aforementioned prince and marquis, have a particularly sadistic streak to your personality, you might want to offer to assist your new consortium partners in getting their automated system up and running. Even more amazing, you can watch them slowly struggle and suffer, offering sage advice meanwhile, and later they will even thank you for it. Even better, you might want to go into automation consulting and get *paid* to do these things. Wouldn't the divine marquis be jealous!

References

Tang, Y.M., and Robin Su. *Social Hygienic Handbook: Government Formulary.* http://www.hkma.com.hk/std/govert.html

Chapter 2

Libraries, Libertarianism and the State

"Librarianship has for its purpose the maintenance of the part of the life of the individual which is the activity of thinking freely."
— A. Broadfield
A Philosophy of Librarianship
(1949)

1. Introduction.

A common characteristic of most librarians is a healthy respect for, and sometimes even an unwholesome desire for, good books. Most of us love a good book the way Ben Jonson loved wine, whether it is good for us or not. We read voraciously, as if searching for something precious that we have lost. And yet, despite the enormous number of new books published each year, it is rare to discover a book that speaks to a reader with a clarity of purpose and a genuine wisdom that overshadows the dull, lazy verbosity of most "philosophical" literature. In this age, it seems that the more vague and shadowy the ideas, the greater respect given by scholars to a work of philosophy. What passes for "professional literature" is usually dull and boring. And so it is a delight to discover not only a good book, but a book which casts a beam of light into the shadows, and creates clarity in an area where the muck of obscure ideas and lazy prose has created only darkness and void.

In my own lifetime, I have found a few books that have given me pleasure through the discovery of new ideas. For me, many of these books were novels, including books like Herman Melville's *The Confidence Man* or Robert Anton Wilson's *The Illuminatus Trilogy*. Sometimes even violent and "pornographic" books, like Tom Walmsley's *Shades* or Stewart Home's *No Pity*, can contain a core of truth that redeems the rest of the book. Frankly, I have a pretty strong stomach and, until recently, I've never had to stop reading a book because of its graphic descriptions. The exception to this is Samuel Delany's novel *Mad Man*, which is well-written but just too bizarre, even for me (and I'm the guy who sat in the back of a movie theater in Washington, D.C., laughing through the whole second half of the Roman Polanski film *Bitter Moon*). Actually, this probably says a great deal about our culture, that it's easier for many of us to accept (or even appreciate) the sadistic violence of *No Pity*, rather than experience (even vicariously) the peculiar masochistic sexual extremes of *Mad Man*.

But the vast majority of novels, good or otherwise, are not novels of ideas. As much as you might enjoy reading *Gone with the Wind*, books like these serve only to entertain us for a few moments, especially popular romance novels and most genre fiction. And so, like *Dangerous Liaisons*, they may give us pleasure, all too fleeting, but they do not advance our thoughts, except indirectly by exposing us to people and situations different from our own. They may encourage empathy with other people and cultures, but they do not inspire thought.

The books that have changed my thinking the most are the ones that challenged my way of seeing the world. In fact, if a book does not radically alter your way of viewing the world, the book has failed in its purpose, or worse yet it has simply served to reinforce your already predigested notions, derived from public school textbooks, Sunday school, and network television news, not to mention other media outlets — meaning the vastly powerful entertainment conglomerates like Disney, Time/Warner, or worse yet *Reader's Digest*. In fact, for many middle-class families, their conception of the world bears as much similarity to the real world as Disneyland's "Pirates of the Caribbean" ride is similar to the experience of being carjacked or mugged.

My own favorite books include Michael Bakunin's *God and the State*, Edgar Wind's *Pagan Mysteries in the Renaissance*, Morton Smith's *Jesus the Magician*, and Jacques Lacarriere's *The Gnostics*. The only book of library science to make the list is A. Broadfield's *A Philosophy of Librarianship*. This is because most library science texts are not about ideas, but about techniques, focused mainly on the "How to" side of our profession. In the library profession, the theory of *why* we do what we do has been sadly overlooked. The establishment of various recommendations and policies is the closest we usually come to actually putting forth a philosophy of Librarianship.

As a matter of practice, most librarians function out of either liberalism or good old American-style pragmatism, depending on the kind of political pressures, good or bad, that are being brought to bear on the library from outside agencies, including library boards and local governments.

Most university libraries function with a philosophy which I would call Machiavellian liberalism. By "Machiavellian liberalism" I mean that most academic librarians tend to disguise their actions in the language of "liberalism" while actually doing whatever it takes to claw, bite, and scratch their way to the top of the academic heap, climbing over the backs of fellow librarians. Private colleges and universities, being somewhat more conservative, usually appeal to traditional "Christian" or "humanistic" values when they stab you in the back, Sir Thomas More–style. Having served on the university's Faculty Affairs Committee, I've seen how some faculty subtly manage to sabotage requests for funding from professors they don't like. I recall one professor not showing up for a meeting so that she wouldn't have to argue in favor of a sabbatical request made by a professor in her own department. The political game is played in libraries just as it is in other departments on campus. Either way, as my old English professor taught me in his Shakespeare seminar, "It is better to be vile than vile esteemed." This dictum is the order of the day, meaning "do what you have to do; just make it look good!" or in Gen X talk: "Just do it!"

A. Broadfield's *A Philosophy of Librarianship* (1949) puts forth a philosophy that goes beyond conventional political philosophies, embracing a libertarian vision that saw far beyond the conflicts of the day. Writing at the end of World War II, Broadfield saw clearly the results of fascism and communism, and decided to forge a philosophy of librarianship based on rejecting all authoritarian tendencies, including these tendencies as they existed in the prevailing liberalism and pragmatism of his day. This meant rejecting the traditional justifications for why societies bother to create libraries, including the desire to "improve" and assimilate the immigrant working classes. Broadfield's main concern is with the idea of freedom, revealed in his statement, "One of the main causes of the misery of man in society is the inability of human beings to do without government. The problem is to discover how they can be governed and yet free" (page 11). He saw that, while it is the responsibility of political philosophers to discover how we can best restrain government and society from encroaching on our lives and actions, it is the special province of librarians to defend and advance the freedom of ideas.

In spite of all the guarantees given us under the Bill of Rights, defending the freedom of ideas is still an enormous challenge. We have, as a nation, made some little progress in this area, but we have not yet even begun to seriously address the larger issues of freedom of action. Freedom of ideas is the first step in a long series of steps toward ensuring personal freedom. And each time we think we are solidly planted on that first step and ready for the next, a new challenge forces us back down. The Constitutional principles of freedom of religion, freedom of speech, and freedom of the press have not advanced much in the last twenty years. In some cases they have been seriously hedged or badly compromised, as with the corporate takeover of many small community newspapers (Hellinger and Judd's *The Democratic Facade* gives a good short summary of these and other current political problems). Even more frightening, from the standpoint of libraries, is the way a few large publishers have come to almost completely dominate the publishing field, so that new information and ideas which might challenge the "corporate wisdom" of The Media are being shoved even further toward the margins.

It is unsettling to see our neighbors, day after day, trying to function as if we had really already realized the 18th century dream of creating a society governed by law and peopled with rational "citizens" in a free and independent country. For many of us this delusion is difficult to maintain while we are under the constant manipulation of Wall Street and Madison Avenue. What is even more frightening is the fact that most of our neighbors gladly accept this situation and only wish to extend the power of these giant corporations into Third-World countries. Apparently, it is easier to be a slave if everyone is a slave. This is the basic psychological justification of fascism.

It is the responsibility of the librarian to help people to think more clearly, which is exactly the opposite of the goal of Madison Avenue. We try to act as if the 18th century goal of creating a "rational" society is, in fact, attainable. And we often do this, flying in the face of evidence that humans are not particularly rational, let alone capable of resisting the propaganda blasted at them, day in and day out, from the print and electronic media. Unfortunately, in many communities the library has become little more than another vehicle for electronic and print messages coming from Madison Avenue. Most of our periodicals seem to be little more than vehicles for advertising. For magazines like *Time* and *Newsweek*, the news story is just the paper wrapped around the dead fish — news is the medium and advertising is the message. Which deodorant you will buy today is the only real concern of advertisers. For modern journalists, the "marketplace of ideas" refers mainly to the power of advertisers to determine our "choices" as we are bought and sold as consumers. This "marketplace" was once an idealistic view about the free exchange of ideas between rational beings; but that idea is long gone, just as the quaint 18th century concepts of "democracy" and "republican government" have gone the way of the dinosaur.

News is just another vehicle for advertising, and even the news itself has usually been cribbed from position papers put out by corporations, government agencies, and other special interest groups. Our own professional library journals have come to look just like the professional journals put out for hair stylists, doctors, and even sanitation engineers, with lots of glossy advertisements. Every time I see an advertisement with a library director giving a glowing testimonial to a particular automated library system, or worse yet, to a book vendor who I know is actively working to destroy librarianship as a profession, I stop and pinch myself, saying: "Am I dreaming, or is this guy nuts?"

The library should aim toward providing the educational materials for creating a rational citizen, but this goal is often co-opted by a wide range of other goals forced on us by the community, including providing light reading, movie videos, music, stock market reports and investment information, addresses and phone numbers, and now even access to the internet, not to mention all of our youth-oriented social agendas. This obsession with "correcting" social problems has already completely overrun public education, so that students and teachers are forced to engage in a thousand little tasks that have nothing to do with creating an enlightened citizenry. In a sense, schools and libraries have become "correctional institutions." In much the same way "gifted" education in our schools has been completely co-opted by "special" education and all of its enormous financial demands. The goal of helping to promote rational thought and discourse has been lost in the shuffle.

In fact, many powerful institutions are struggling against us, trying to prevent the growth of an enlightened citizenry. Both governments and corporations see the creation of citizens capable of making reasoned judgments and rational decisions as a direct threat to their own agendas. A rational person is not easily led and manipulated, let alone controlled. Broadfield was well aware of the efforts of government to make decisions for us, saying, "For society, acting as it may be supposed through government, has not the right to decide how a man shall be used, and it is better that he should retain the right to waste his own life than that his abilities and activities should pass under the forceful protection of society" (page 17). Today, of course, an even greater threat to our autonomy is advertising, where we are "persuaded" to waste our lives in a way that makes as much money as possible for someone else, or subtly encouraged to make political changes that will benefit one special interest or another. Emotional manipulation and public opinion polls are the basis of public policy today, not reasoned debate.

At the same time, libraries are subject to the same market forces as individuals, not to mention the political forces that originally brought the library into being and the economic forces that help to maintain us as institutions. Most libraries are maintained primarily through taxation, and only marginally through fees and fines. We serve the will of the majority of tax-payers, over the objection of those citizens who do not use and do not want to pay for our services.

Keeping this always in mind, we have a responsibility to collect books widely, so that the library represents the widest possible range of view-points. Generally speaking, these books fall into three categories:

1. The books and resources you need to provide.
2. The books and resources you want to provide.
3. The rest of it.

Category 1 must be covered, if you are to provide a basic, minimum level of service. Category 2 is covered, if and when money is left over from what you spend on 1. And category 3 is all the other odds and ends that the rest of the library staff thinks you need to buy, whether you agree the purchase is a good idea or not.

Your primary interest is, of course, with category 2. That is where you justify buying materials that will promote the growth of sovereign indi-viduals and the creation of an enlightened republic. The question now is: How are you going to locate these materials?

2. What Is Truth?

Ultimately, libraries are involved in the quest for truth. But we approach this issue in a way that is very different from most institutions. Most people concern themselves with discovering "Truth" in an exclusive way, trying to separate the wheat from the chaff. Libraries, however, use an inclusive technique, trying to include as many different versions of "Truth" as possible, in the hopes that somewhere in the mass of material, some truth may be found by the discerning reader. At one time this job seemed much simpler. The total quantity of material to be collected was much smaller, and a person of independent means, like Thomas Jefferson, could afford to collect a fair amount of "Truth" in his own personal library. But just as Mr. Jefferson's library has grown, mutated, and transformed itself over the years, becoming the vast holdings of the Library of Congress, the sheer quantity of "Truth" has expanded in recent years to the point where it now threatens to overwhelm even the largest of research libraries.

If, however, we decide to exclude "information" from what we call "Truth," it may be that there really is no more truth in existence now than there was when the Buddha sat under his tree and contemplated the universe.

The mass of data has grown to overshadow truth, so that we often lose sight of what is important.

The librarian's role has shifted, as the amount of informational data has grown to the point that now we are certain to exclude a lot more material than we add, simply because of the limits of resources of space, labor, and money available to us. We now exclude a lot more material than we could ever possibly include. For this reason, libraries have been forced to rely heavily on book review journals to help us make decisions about what to buy.

At one time, librarians were able to rely on review journals to function independently from the publishers who produced the books. But because of market forces, review journals have come to rely very heavily on advertising dollars, to the extent that they can no longer legitimately claim to be free of financial ties to the publishers who buy advertising in their publications. Once upon a time, you could expect a review journal to present a somewhat unbiased view. Today, however, review journals function more frequently as paid "infomercials" to assist in the transfer of library dollars to the media conglomerates they serve.

The influence of the large corporate publishers is so great that reviewers, and companies that perform "review" functions, have trouble directly opposing them, let alone performing a "critic's" function. For example, Baker & Taylor Link shows Bret Easton Ellis's violent novel *American Psycho* to be appropriate for "B&T School Selection Guide 7–12 Titles to Order [1992]." Do they honestly believe this book should be recommended for high school students? Or is this just more evidence of the power of the large commercial publishers to quietly "influence" both reviewers and vendors?

A further issue is how publishers use review journals as a source for "blurbs"—short quotations from reviews that go on book covers or dust jackets. I suspect that a statistical analysis of these reviews would show that large commercial publishers get many more "positive" words and phrases, even in overtly critical reviews, while small presses get few positive words or phrases that might be quoted in blurbs.

This problem has been made even more acute as review journals have moved from reviewing titles after they are published to reviewing proof sheets of books before they are even printed. Several influential review journals demand that publishers provide them with proof sheets *before* the book is published if they want to get reviewed at all. As a result of this policy, they have also shifted more toward having professional staff on site "evaluate" the books, rather than automatically farming the books out for review to "amateur" reviewers. Many times the decision to review (or not review) a book is made before a reasonable evaluation of the quality of the book can be determined. And usually this means that commercial presses, and especially those that now, or are soon likely to, buy advertising in these journals, are usually given "the benefit of the doubt" as to the quality of their books.

This seems to be the justification for prepublication announcements that appear in some review journals. And when (surprise! surprise!) these same books become bestsellers, that then is the justification for using prepublication announcements, approval plans, and a whole host of labor-saving practices that are designed to make life easier for the librarians, while simplifying the process of transferring money into the pockets of book vendors.

In some cases a book is "recommended" for purchase based on issues totally unrelated to the quality of the book, but important to marketing, including the size of the advertising budget. For example, Martin Marzarala, Manager of Collection Development Services for Baker & Taylor, in a recent editorial suggested that B&T was qualified to make better decisions about collection development for libraries because B&T has access to vital information, including "two key attributes frequently neglected in popular journals, namely first print run and advertising budget." Baker & Taylor would use these two criteria heavily because, as Mr. Marzarala says, "Why wait for a review when much could be gained by relying on other equally valuable selection criteria?" Using these criteria obviously skews the selection process toward the big commercial publishers. And I don't think anyone would question the idea that B&T would prefer promoting the commercial products of the big New York concerns, rather than having to deal with thousands of small and independent presses.

If review journals really wanted to make their reviews more independent and impartial they could (1) go back to reviewing books *after* they are published, and (2) try to rely on a wider, more diverse range of subject specialists. In an ideal world, review journals would make the effort to review as much material as possible within their area of coverage, even if the review is quite brief, and then send a copy of the review to the publisher, whether or not the review is ever published. The publisher could then quote from that unpublished review for blurbs, and citing the reviewer by name. For example:

> "Exciting style…"
> —Joe Blow, reviewer for *Books on Your List.*

This way, even smaller presses would have the benefit of a promotional blurb in marketing their books. Of course, no review journal would ever do this, as it would tend to decrease the value of a published review in their journal. After all, what we are talking about here is the exchange of published reviews for advertiser's dollars. No editor for a "commercial" book review journal would jeopardize that relationship by giving them away for free.

To test this theory, I recently examined a small sample of reviews from one of the prestigious review journals and compared the reviews for books published by companies that advertise in the journal with reviews for books published by companies that didn't advertise in the journal. Using this blunt instrument, I could not find evidence of bias in the language used in the reviews. I did, however, note that, although buying advertising in the journal did not guarantee a good review, it did seem to protect you from getting a bad review. All of the "bad" reviews were given to book publishers who did not buy advertising in the review journal. Obviously, more research is needed in this area, to find if there is bias in the way reviews are "awarded."

To complicate the search for "Truth" even more, whole industries have grown up around developing and perfecting ways to lie to the public. Several scholars have already explored how the news media distort the truth. Michael Parenti in *Inventing Reality: The Politics of News Media* and Paul Weaver in *News and the Culture of Lying* have documented how this has developed over the last century within journalism, but the ongoing program of lies and manipulation is much older than that. The systematic manipulation and falsification of "Truth" by institutions is as old as history.

During the period beginning with World War I, and rapidly accelerating during World War II, a variety of new techniques were developed for manipulating public opinion. Today, the public quite naturally assumes it is being lied to, every time someone steps in front of a microphone. The public is becoming more and more cynical, and rightly so, about public discourse. At the same time, and perhaps as a result, it seems as if there is a whole new industry being created around books that expose the fallacies of the past, including such titles as *Lies My Teacher Told Me* by James W. Loewen, *Don't Know Much about the Civil War* by Kenneth C. Davis, *Deceptions and Myths of the Bible* by Lloyd M. Graham, *The Jesus Conspiracy* by Holger Kersten, and *Legends, Lies and Cherished Myths of World History* by Richard Shenkman.

Although the lies of the past are sometimes discovered by modern scholars, most contemporary scholarship in the liberal arts is devoted, not to a search for truth, but to newer and newer reinterpretations of already existing material, with each new reinterpretation becoming more and more embellished and encumbered with the latest critical techniques, including the popular avant-garde French or Russian theories of critical "discourse" — a euphemism for murky prose and bizarre psychological speculations. Most of this scholarship avoids making a statement of fact that could be supported by evidence. That would be too dangerous, as evidence can be disproved.

For example, a book of literary criticism, published several years ago, made the claim that women's writing had a distinct quality that distinguished it from writing by men. The touchstone of this book was a short story by an "anonymous" 19th century woman. This book became very popular among academic feminists, and it was only recently discovered that the anonymous 19th century woman was neither anonymous nor a woman: "She" was actually Washington Irving. This revelation has not dampened the enthusiasm of some feminists though, who still believe that "female" writing is a tangible, material reality that exists apart and can be studied independently from "male" writing.

Complicating the issue even more is the way that "truth" is reported selectively — so that history is falsified by the misreporting of truth. This problem is fairly chronic in books published by university presses. For example, a recent scholarly book on the presidential campaign of 1992 in Missouri failed to mention the controversy over the illegal ways the Bush campaign dealt with anti–Bush protesters in Branson and Joplin. This information was widely reported in the local press and even found its way into an article in the *New Republic*, but it was not mentioned in a university press book analyzing the campaign in Missouri. I would suggest that, at least in this case, the truth was marginalized out of existence. There is a similar problem with *Kansas: A Bicentennial History* by Kenneth Davis. This book, published with support from the federal government, manages to cover "Bleeding Kansas" and Prohibition, which are usually covered in high school textbooks, and the author positively gushes over editor William Allen White. Yet somehow the book fails to mention J.A. Wayland and the *Appeal to Reason* newspaper or E. Haldeman-Julius and his Little Blue Book publishing company, both of which had far more impact nationwide than White did. But, because of their ties to socialism and free thought, both Wayland and Haldeman-Julius have been marginalized out of Kansas history.

In some cases, these scholarly books represent what could only be described as a "whitewash" of history. For example, several university presses have recently published books that try to "improve" the history of the Catholic missions in South America. It seems to me rather odd that political writers in the 19th century would use the Jesuit missions in

Paraguay as an example, the readiest that came to mind, of a native population ground under the heel of religious bigotry and political oppression. And yet today, historians describe these same missions as a kind of "utopia" in the New World, run by the enlightened Jesuit fathers. In many cases, it seems that these "scholars" focus so tightly on a specific set of facts that they fail to see the bigger picture, and so serve up a misrepresentation of history. This whitewashed version of history has already found its way into popular culture through the film *The Mission* (1986).

There are, however, a few exceptions to this rule about university press books, including for example Davis Joyce's *An Oklahoma I Had Never Seen Before*, which, although published by a university press, does give an "alternative" history of the state that is quite different from what you find in textbooks. History can be interesting, in spite of what you often find coming out of university presses.

It's not that I expect (or want) every history book to be written like John Reed's *Ten Days That Shook the World*, but it would be nice to see history recorded with a little more passion and interest in the events being described. History is often marginalized by being made boring.

This process of maginalizing protest is also reflected in the way review journals handle controversial books. More often than not, reviewers tend to support the currently orthodox ideas. For example, a book critical of Alcoholics Anonymous, called *Alcoholics Anonymous: Cult or Cure?*, was sent by one of the major review journals to a supporter of AA for review. Needless to say, the reviewer tore the book to shreds in her review. The AA establishment, like most religious orthodoxies, is not to be trifled with!

Sometimes a book can be so dangerous, politically, that ignoring it is not enough — it has to be actively suppressed by the establishment. This was the case with the recent publication of the original, unexpurgated version of the classic American novel *The Jungle*, now called *The Lost First Edition of Upton Sinclair's The Jungle*.

In the earlier 1906 version of *The Jungle*, many of Upton Sinclair's graphic descriptions of the Chicago meatpacking industry were cut out of the manuscript at the demand of the publisher. Almost a third of the book was cut, and words like "bloody" were changed to "red" throughout the book to lessen its impact. But even this emasculated version of *The Jungle* was horrific enough in its descriptions of unsanitary Chicago slaughterhouses to bring pressure to bear for the passage of the federal pure food legislation.

Unfortunately, the rediscovery and publication of this "lost" version of Sinclair's *Jungle* came at the same time as an effort by the Bush Administration to weaken federal meat inspection standards. They were worried that this newly restored *Jungle* would wreck their plans to further weaken the inspection of meats required by the pure food laws. And so the original uncut version of *The Jungle* was quickly sandbagged by people with ties to the meatpacking industry. Luckily for President Bush, the meatpacking industry was able to crush the book before it really got rolling.

Discovering the truth, the little bits and pieces that trickle down from the corporate mega-media conglomerates, let alone trying to collect it, is the most serious challenge for libraries today. Sifting out the little pieces of truth, while trying to ignore the din from scandals and media events, is very difficult. Real human suffering is covered up by the media event of Princess Diana's untimely (though hardly "tragic") death. Real issues of political corruption evaporate in the growing shadows of the Clinton sex scandals. The problem of a failing legal system is harshly mocked by the O.J. Simpson trial. Given the media's overwhelming obsession with celebrity, it's hardly surprising that the truth gets pushed to the margins. With the overwhelming power of today's electronic media, it is harder to locate and identify truth than it was in the harshest years of Stalin's empire.

3. Freedom, Just Another Word...

In examining the (almost) prevailing authoritarianism that existed in Europe at the end of World War II, A. Broadfield struggled with the idea of how a library should function. On the one hand, libraries exist as the product of government, as one of many services provided to its citizens. On the other hand, libraries should be working to bring into being individuals who can think for themselves, even if that means that they work to oppose or even to overthrow the existing government. A perfect example of this case is when Karl Marx made extensive use of British libraries while writing his political and economic works. It is one of the ironies of intellectual freedom that we provide information and services that work against our own political interests. The people who work for the Congressional Research Service must face this dilemma fairly often.

In addition to helping to form individuals who can, in effect, "stand alone" within the social order, libraries also work to instill in people a recognition of ethical standards, including the responsibility to consider the needs of others. Disregarding the needs of others should be contrary to the goals of an enlightened and rational citizen. Only the most radical form of egoist believes that we should try to exist outside and apart from human society.

More frequently, it is the society that tries to force its views onto the individual. The individual can resist, and in many cases has a moral duty to resist. Hopefully, some day we will no longer have to deal with authoritarian institutions and the political forces that breed them. As Broadfield pointed out, "The ultimate objective is not the *surrender* of tyrannical power, but its prevention, since liberty is not conceded to the individual by authority, but conceded to authority by the individual..." (page 24). Broadfield goes on to compare librarians, who sometimes use their positions to push material onto their patrons, to bureaucrats promoting a slum clearance program. That is, you can move people out of their homes against their will, but you can't make them like it.

Some ideas are fragile things, and they cannot be forced into existence, any more than you can create a community by force. Other ideas are quite durable, and they resist being completely crushed, no matter how powerful the censors are. It is interesting to note, too, what kind of experiences can bring an idea into existence. It is possible to experience a moment of enlightenment while watching an old horror movie on television. That people continue to experience moments of truth, in spite of our media-manipulated society, points up the fact that it is difficult for a library to serve its authoritarian masters very well. Keeping out material that critiques its political masters is almost impossible. Messages may have to be disguised to get by the censors, but they will get by.

Similarly, a librarian can have lots of high ideas about improving the reading habits of a community, but if they don't like what you're shoveling, they won't stop at the library. People come to have ideas in very strange ways, and we are not in the business of manipulating this process, at least not directly. A librarian may turn a library into a museum of enlightenment, full of goodness and light. But the people who need the enlightenment most will usually be standing around the corner, watching a cockfight. The goal of the library should be to create an intellectual environment that encourages learning, and especially independent thinking, while avoiding the role of being merely an instrument for authoritarian control.

Broadfield is especially disturbed by the idea that libraries might some day come under a central control. "For then the reader gets what the central controller intends that he should get, and the central controller makes common cause with others like himself in other departments of public life, so as to promote the maximum homogeneity and efficiency" (page 26). We have not yet attained this level of control in the West, though it may have existed briefly in some communist countries. However, we do have forces that move us in this general direction, though by using market forces rather than through direct government control.

One trend toward greater centralization and control is the use of "outsourcing" to replace traditional library functions. Librarians are becoming increasingly concerned about this trend, and with good reason. It was a matter of concern when libraries began outsourcing their cataloging. With the outsourcing of acquisitions, and, in some cases, almost all library functions, this trend threatens the existence of "librarianship" as a profession. The economic pressure to cut costs is taking a terrible toll on libraries and on the library mission in our communities. It's easy to see how, once acquisitions and public services are controlled remotely, by a corporation whose headquarters is located thousands of miles away, the homogenization of our culture will only accelerate at an even faster pace.

For a vendor, owned and controlled by a larger corporation, the ideals of librarianship are irrelevant. A vendor believes that it is providing adequate library service as long as the current bestsellers are in the library and circulation statistics are high. These goals are not far removed from the goals of some librarians who are obsessed with circulation statistics (as if service to the community could be measured by these numbers). But "good" statistics should not be the goal of the profession. Just as accountants, lawyers, and doctors have standards of professional conduct, librarians should have standards that point beyond providing patrons with current bestsellers.

In a related trend, many libraries are moving toward greater and greater use of vendor-supplied CD products for collection development. Unfortunately, these products tend to focus on materials published by big publishers and ignore small and medium-sized presses. The vendors use the excuse that this proves they are "selective" in the book titles they choose to add. Most of these CD products include reviews from *Booklist* or *Publishers Weekly/Library Journal*, which again tends to focus the attention of librarians who use these CD products toward big commercial publishers. And, for small presses, being lucky enough to get a review in *Library Journal* doesn't necessarily mean that your book will be listed in any of these CD products, as even the reviews can often be excluded for reasons of "selectivity" and "quality."

Various collection development tools, in combination with the practices of the Library of Congress (in particular the CIP, or Cataloguing-in-Publication program), tend to push bookstores and libraries toward making selections in a particular way. Homogeneity is created, just as in the Eastern-bloc countries, but in our case through the use of market forces rather than authoritarian control. The result, however, is pretty much the same, so that all the chain bookstores in the mall have pretty much the same books in stock, as part of the "chains" of capitalism. The selection of music in discount stores is even more standardized, so that the difference from one Wal-Mart to the next is almost nonexistent. The not-so-invisible hand of the market now controls most of our selections. And if the indirect controls are not enough, we can count on the media to ballyhoo the latest Stephen King novel or Rush Limbaugh book to the point where library patrons are practically breaking down the door to get at them.

The problem is, of course, that the big commercial publishers are pretty sure of what we will buy. Or at least they are pretty sure that they can persuade us, with a large enough advertising budget, to read a particular book through a well-planned marketing campaign. This kind of thinking rarely goes wrong, and when it does (as with the Dolly Parton autobiography) it becomes newsworthy as an aberration in the book markets. Publishers rarely lose money by overestimating the power of advertising.

Actually, most publishers don't really care if we actually read their books or not, as long as we buy a copy. I'm convinced that the number of people who actually read *The Name of the Rose*, for example, is exceeded by far by the number of people who bought a copy. The same is true for Rush Limbaugh's books, and for a whole list of bestsellers that many people buy, but few people actually read all the way through. Big, commercial publishers sometimes have to rely heavily on the herd instinct to rack up sales. How else could you sell thousands of copies of such mediocre works as *The Closing of the American Mind*? Or, worse yet, a whole array of genre novels, which a generation ago would have had trouble getting printed in hard covers, let alone promoted by reputable bookstores and book clubs.

In fact, the commercial success of a book often depends on its promoting certain political views. A number of books have become bestsellers based only on the fact that they promote a point of view which is popular with the Left or the Right and have a large number of readers primed and ready to accept the book's arguments, no matter how poorly reasoned and presented. It helps if the author is a controversial political figure like former Education Secretary William Bennett. His bestseller *The De-Valuing of America* presents a catalog of political orthodoxies that ring true with his constituency, but it offers little except anecdotal evidence for proof, in a manner perfected by the *Reader's Digest* "school" of journalism.

Again, Allan Bloom's *The Closing of the American Mind* is a good example of a book with a political agenda whose line of argument is laughable. The audience for this book didn't really care about the arguments; they were already primed and ready to believe anything the author said. Bloom's book has been widely criticized by academics (see Howard Bloom's *The Lucifer Principle* for a more complete critique), but these attacks have had little effect on the popularity of the book. Of course the grand champion of this whole genre is James Burnham. His book *The Suicide of the West* makes the argument, based on the changing colors of a political atlas, that Western democracies have committed suicide and worldwide communism is only a small step away from victory over a prostrate Europe and an enfeebled America. History, however, has demonstrated that freedom and slavery are not easily contained by the colors and lines drawn on a map.

Unfortunately, we tend to buy books that reinforce our preconceived notions, half-digested thoughts, and personal biases. The books that try to challenge these beliefs usually fail miserably. On those occasions when new ideas catch fire, I am convinced that it is because a fair number of people have already recognized that their old ideas were mistaken and they are out there looking for a new idea, or perhaps just a way to retread an old idea. It's amazing how popular a retread can be! How else can you explain the enormous success of John Gray's *Mars and Venus in the Bedroom*? This book is full of trite old ideas that no one in his or her right mind could take seriously. Yet Gray cranks out these Mars and Venus books on a regular schedule, sells videos and does seminars, as if he really had a new idea. Gray's series of Mars and Venus books reinforces a set of stereotypes that should have died out a decade ago, yet he still produces the bestsellers.

At the same time, a really remarkable book like Kate Fillion's *Lip Service*, which deals with female social relationships in a positive way, has trouble staying in print for a year and is quickly remaindered and swept under the rug. Unlike Gray, Fillion approaches the subject of relationships and gender communication using recent research and a genuine insight into how people think. And it ends up on the sale table of remaindered books. Go figure!

It's also true that, once an author has a successful book, the author's publisher tends to stick with him, no matter what. After the controversy over Bret Easton Ellis's *American Psycho*, Knopf brought out his *The Informers* with a dust jacket covered with blurbs praising *American Psycho*. The publisher's claim, based on the blurbs, is that Ellis is a satirist who is simply misunderstood. Taking the publisher at its word, I read *The Informers* and found it a depressing, cynical, meandering tale consisting of episodes in the lives of various West Coast characters. The satire, if it is satire, shows the shallowness of their lives. It also includes several vampires (so it wasn't a total waste of time, for me anyway). I have trouble understanding how this is satire, since there is no sense that there is some other set of values these characters could live by. In my humble opinion, *The Informers* is no more a satire than Pat Booth's *All for Love*. Ellis ought to go to

Hollywood and write screenplays, or maybe get a job writing for the television series *Silk Stalkings*. Such powerful and all-encompassing shallowness shouldn't go to waste in mere novels.

4. The Slavery of Our Cherished Beliefs.

In addition to criticizing the trend toward centralization and centralized decision-making, Broadfield's *A Philosophy of Librarianship* set forth ideas on how a library should serve its educational function. For example, Broadfield criticizes educational programs, saying that they "achieve only a limited success in the effort to show people how to set about finding truth. Instead they aim to impart supposed facts" (page 42). Broadfield further claims that these "facts" are really no more than dogmas, and usually dogmas "selected as such, with the purpose of inducing the governed to take the same view of what they ought to do and desire as the legislators" (page 42).

The idea that a school or a library should teach students how to find truth, irrespective of how it relates to our "national heritage," would probably strike terror into the hearts of most politicians. Witness the controversy over the Hiroshima display that was to be presented at the Smithsonian a few years ago. Veterans groups, combined with conservative legislators, were able to block the display, claiming it was somehow unfair to veterans. In fact, one wonders what horrified them more: Was it the visible evidence in photographic displays of the effect of an atomic bomb on a civilian population? Or was it the idea that the average citizen might be led to question the original decision to drop the bomb? Or, worse yet, was it that citizens might feel they have not only the right but the responsibility to question the decisions made by their leaders?

We are indoctrinated into these cherished beliefs from an early age. As most of us grew up, we were taught to swear allegiance to the United States through "The Pledge of Allegiance." Since then, many of us have come to question the purpose embodied in that oath. I first began to question the purpose for the oath when I discovered that the phrase "under God" was inserted into the line "one nation, indivisible" by an act of Congress in 1952. After I discovered that fact, I began omitting this phrase when I was asked to recite the oath. Later, when I discovered that the oath came into being shortly after the end of the Civil War, I came to question the purpose of the rest of that line. And every time the Pat Robertsons and Jerry Falwells of the world use the Pledge of Allegiance as a justification for forcing their own religious values down our throats, I get the urge to burn a flag or two.

Perhaps I'm taking this all too personally. It is something of a "family matter," as I've always taken a certain amount of pride in the role the Lee family has played in the American Revolution. As a college student, I could point with pride to the fact that Richard Henry Lee was a signer of the Declaration of Independence. At the same time, I was puzzled about the fact that, although he was a prominent leader under the Articles of Confederation, he was not one of the signers of the Constitution. It wasn't until after I graduated from college that I discovered that Richard Henry Lee was an Anti-Federalist and one of the leaders of the opposition to the Constitution! And, more important, it was the opposition of R.H. Lee and others that forced the Federalists to add a Bill of Rights to the Constitution. Originally, the promoters of the Constitution argued strongly against adding a Bill of Rights altogether!

The fact that many leaders of the American Revolution opposed the Constitution is something that you rarely ever learn about in college, let alone high school history classes. The writers of history textbooks apparently feel that it is important for students to see the establishment of this country as a united effort, including the adoption of the Constitution. And I'm sure the writers of textbooks in the 21st century will approach the passage of NAFTA in much the same spirit.

One way that textbook authors have falsified our history is in the selective approach they take to the American Revolution. Most authors spend a great deal of time discussing the *Federalist Papers*, which, if they were honest, would more rightly be classified as part of the postwar reaction against the Revolution. Try imagining the textbooks of the 22nd century discussing the Reagan era as if it were a part of the student movements of the sixties. Better yet, imagine historians of the future reading Newt Gingrich's *Contract with America* to get a better understanding of the political philosophy of the sixties!

At the same time, historians neglect America's libertarian heritage, including the writings of Algernon Sidney and Joseph Priestley, and such vital documents as *Cato's Letters*, written by Trenchard and Gordon earlier in the 18th century. The revolutionary leaders, from Franklin to Jefferson, recommended *Cato's Letters* to anyone who wanted to understand what the American Revolution was all about. But most history books dealing with the Revolution, including popular works like Gary Wills' *Inventing America*, don't even bother to mention *Cato's Letters*, instead focusing on the more "politically correct" writings of John Locke or *The Federalist Papers*. Similarly, historians who study our legal system tend to focus on the influence of Blackstone's *Commentaries on the Laws of England*, rather than on the more libertarian legal commentaries that were popular with Thomas

Jefferson and his contemporaries. There are very few books written about the alternatives to Federalism, and the ones that are available, like Wilson McWilliams' *The Federalists, the Antifederalists, and the American Political Tradition*, are geared toward an audience of scholars rather than the general public. It is hard to imagine a nation where the average citizens are more ignorant of their own history than we are. And this is largely the fault of our textbooks.

The American Revolution pretty much ended with the adoption of the Constitution, and the Rule of Law in this country ended when President Andrew Jackson chose to ignore the decision of the Supreme Court and sent thousands of Cherokees on a forced death march, in what has since become known as the Trail of Tears. Similarly, the Civil War marked the end of political and economic regionalism in this country. Some people think that the Civil War marked the end of slavery. Rather, the Civil War was a particularly violent and brutal military action that determined whether black Americans would remain chattel slaves on Southern farms or be given the opportunity to become wage slaves in Northern factories. The Civil War did not end slavery; it simply determined what shape and form that slavery would take for future generations. Politically, the Civil War firmly established federal power as dominant over state power.

Much the same process has taken place in our understanding of our religious heritage. Centuries of bloody repressions are largely passed over in our history books as if they never happened. Most of our so-called founding fathers were well aware of the dangers of religious controversy. Because we have dumbed-down and falsified our own history, we have difficulty understanding, let alone coming to grips with, the bloody warfare between the various branches of Islam in the Middle East, not to mention the mass murder in Bosnia. Worse yet, we tend to view the Holocaust as if it were an aberration, a moral lapse of the German leadership, rather than the inevitable cultural product of centuries of anti–Semitism.

Mostly it is due to our own unwillingness to recognize the long history of hatred that exists between the various denominations of Christianity in this country. If "ignorance is bliss," the United States must be the happiest country in the world. The denominations that make up our religious heritage have been in violent conflict for many years, from the persecution of dissenters in New England to the infamous Mormon War of 1838. This is, of course, simply a continuation of a cycle of violence and falsification of church history, going back all the way to its beginnings.

In *The Orthodox Corruption of Scripture: The Effect of Early Christological Controversies on the Text of the New Testament*, Bart Ehrman shows that the early Church fathers regularly altered the gospels in order to "prove" that the "heretics" were wrong. This usually involved altering the scriptures in order to add godlike qualities to a Messiah whose crucifixion had proved him all too human. Erhman proves that such "corruptions" of the scripture were a common method used by the established churches in dealing with heretical ideas.

Of course this is all old news to most biblical scholars. Morton Smith's *Clement of Alexandria and the Secret Gospel of Mark* published the text of a newly-discovered letter written by one of the earliest Church fathers where he directs his followers to lie about the existence of a secret Gospel of Mark. The reason for lying, stated plainly in Clement's letter, was so that orthodox believers could get an advantage over a group of "heretics" who were arguing for a greater acceptance of homosexuals within the early church. Interestingly, Clement's letter quotes the specific passage from the secret gospel that he wanted suppressed, a passage describing a night-time initiation of Lazarus from which he "ran away naked" as soldiers approached. Of course, anyone who tries to engage in a public debate with fundamentalist Christians, arguing for religious toleration and using the Bible as a text, should know that you are playing their game and playing it with a stacked deck. The "Plain Truth" has already gone through two thousand years of heavy massage and manipulation.

Fundamentalist Christians have been particularly angered by efforts of modern scholars to excavate the many layers of massaged text that exist in the Bible. Most fundamentalist interpretations are based on 19th century Victorian ideas, rather than anything in the Bible, but it's hard to convince Christians of this. Most fundamentalists are incapable of making historical judgments or looking at the Bible in a historic context, like the minister who insisted on referring to the King James Bible as the Saint James Bible. Having spent a good many years reading biblical criticism, I feel particularly challenged in approaching a fundamentalist book of "theology" like *Evidence That Demands a Verdict*. This book, a fundamentalist apologetic, clearly shows the conventional fundamentalist perspective on the Bible. That is, every book and gospel was written by the person to whom it is attributed, every jot and tittle is literal and accurate; in spite of the many errors and self-contradictions that exist, it is all literally true. At the other extreme you have the books written for pastors in the so-called "liberal" Christian seminaries. In these textbooks you can see how the author hedges his facts and chooses to phrase questions in a certain way in order to avoid the difficult questions. The naive reader (again, the pastors-in-training) are left with the impression that all is well with the Bible. The authors of these textbooks have avoided the truth, and thus perpetuated a lie, for the greater glory of their particular denomination.

5. *Freud and Truth.*

This process is not exclusive to religion, as most professional bodies have a similar set of holy dogmas that are sacrosanct and above question. In recent years the profession of psychoanalysis has been especially hard-hit, with revelations about Freud and his motivations that are not unlike the revelations made years ago about religious leaders like Joseph Smith, Mary Baker Eddy and Aimee Semple McPherson (see, for example, Paul Kurtz's *The Transcendental Temptation*), and more recently Jim Bakker, Pat Robertson, Madalyn Murray O'Hair, and James Dobson (just to mention a few). Some of the current attacks on the Freudian orthodoxy are coming by way of French intellectual currents, feminism, and even Marxism.

The discovery of "Truth" is often obscured by people who have a vested interest in hiding the facts. For many years access to Freud's private papers has been tightly controlled by a small group of people. The one time they allowed an "outsider" into the archive, the result was Jeffry Masson's controversial book, *The Assault on Truth: Freud's Suppression of the Seduction Theory*. Masson managed to ingratiate himself with the Freudian establishment and to get access to Freud's letters, but what he found was deeply troubling. It appeared that Freud dropped one of his early theories, not because it was psychologically unsound, but because the theory was unpopular, attracting the ire of his fellow doctors.

After his book was published, Masson discovered that the followers of Freud were just as fanatical as the Inquisition in protecting the status quo. In some ways, Masson's career is like that of John Allegro. Allegro, who was a gifted Biblical scholar, criticized the Dead Sea Scroll "mafia" for suppressing the contents of the Dead Sea Scrolls for decades. After publishing several controversial books on this subject, Allegro's career was essentially destroyed. Since then, several other scholars, including Robert Eisenman, have claimed that the contents of the scrolls were suppressed by traditionalist scholars who were concerned about what the scrolls might reveal about the origins of Christianity. Access to the scrolls was limited to scholars who were "reliable"—meaning that they accepted certain preconceived notions about who wrote the scrolls and what they meant.

The fact is that "establishment" scholars prefer to deal with "crackpot" critics like Mary Balmary or B.E. Thiering, whose ideas are so far off-the-wall that they pose no real threat. They prefer this to the criticism of Allegro or Masson, whose ideas—if widely accepted—could upset the applecart, or maybe even clear out the Temple. Generally speaking, "criticism" and "scholarship" that does not fit into certain accepted modes is widely ridiculed. Even works that present innovative approaches to a subject, like Kamal Salabi's *Conspiracy in Jerusalem: The Hidden Origins of Jesus*, may be ignored by the establishment. Salabi, who is a devout Christian, writes from an Arab perspective. And so his ideas are easily sidelined into the "crackpot" category. Critics of the establishment orthodoxy are quickly pushed to the margins.

Broadfield's response to this problem, as put forward in *A Philosophy of Librarianship*, is to make the main function of a library that of providing readers with a collection that includes the widest possible range of opinions. Bluntly stated, this means, "all heterodoxy should be well represented on the library shelves" (pages 42–43), with the goal that the books in a collection *should* contradict each other. Broadfield goes so far as to claim that library education means bringing a patron with firmly-held beliefs to those materials that contradict these beliefs. A library patron should be exposed to material that goes directly counter to the "half-truths" and "falsehoods" instilled in him by schools and the media, with the purpose of teaching the patron to look for truth independently from established sources.

Broadfield specifically suggests that materials be gathered from a variety of countries, in part to provide a variety of opinions, but primarily to show that nationalist biases are all "equally unreliable" (page 43). Although most librarians who try to justify the existence of libraries talk about the "library mission" in the community, Broadfield saw librarianship as an effort to "expose" and discredit all missions, not adding another one to the already bloated list of public goals.

To that extent, libraries are in much the same boat as the Army Corps of Engineers when it proposes doing another water project. When justifying a water project, like damming a river to create a lake, the Corps calculates both the increased value of recreational lands and the control of water supply — two goals that often come into conflict with each other in times of drought or flood. Similarly, the library justifies its existence by both providing support for our heritage and providing material that exposes, challenges and debunks that same supposed heritage. And that is why librarianship is such a schizoid profession. The time has come for us to face the inherent division in our goals, so that we can focus on entering the next century as a truly progressive institution.

6. Market Censorship and the "Outsourcing" Controversy.

The marginalization of small newspapers and magazines, independent bookstores, and small radio stations has increased at an alarming rate.

Today there are few "independent" sources of information left in this country to provide a semblance of "alternative" information. Most of us have been indoctrinated by the media to believe that this is somehow a "good thing" which is supposedly more efficient and streamlined. The upshot is that network news programs nowadays have fewer surprises than the average television game show.

If, in fact, our political culture is based primarily on the concept of the game show, our elections resemble nothing if not professional wrestling. That is, the promoters know the outcome of the contest well ahead of time, but they do their best to make a good show of it, with plenty of screaming and chest-beating, to entertain the rest of us. Just as with the ancient Roman gladiatorial contests, which were slowly corrupted by professionals, our political system has come under the complete control of lobbyists and interest groups. In fact, a recent study found that lobbyists spend over $100 million *a week* to influence Congress. And so these politicians don't have to run for re-election while depending on ten dollar or twenty dollar contributions from the folks back home. Now they can rely on lobbyists to tell them what the folks back home need. In watching modern political contests, you may not know which particular candidate has raised enough money by selling his vote to win the election — the only sure thing is to bet on the lions.

As the game has been fixed, it is the responsibility of the librarian, both as a citizen and as part of the frontline soldier in defending freedom of thought, to find those edges and borders where a certain amount of freedom can successfully be pried loose, to locate the small areas where freedom is still possible. This means finding and providing sources of information that are not corrupted by an authoritarian agenda. Librarians should be looking through book catalogs by alternative presses, like South End Press, or looking at mail order catalogs, like the catalogs put out by Laissez Faire Books, Left Bank Distribution, or AK Press Distribution. Similarly, it is fair to say that a librarian who does book selection should include review sources that cover books published by small presses. Although *Library Journal* and *Booklist* claim to cover small presses, I think a librarian would be well advised to include *Small Press Review*, *Counterpoise*, *MSRRT Newsletter*, and other sources that cover small press books. Librarians must take an active role in finding books that provide alternatives to mass media viewpoints. We should care more about *what* books we provide to the public, and think less about how often it might circulate.

Book vendors, on the other hand, are generally uninterested in what they sell, as long as it sells. For this reason, their goals are quite unrelated to those of the librarian, who is more concerned with what books he or she is providing than with the mark-up. This fact should seem obvious to anyone who thinks about it for more than thirty seconds. Hiring the book vendor to decide which books you will get, while you promise to pay the vendor $20.94 each, is a sure formula for getting a lousy collection of junk books. It's like letting the fox guard the hen house.

Recently Baker & Taylor signed a one-year contract, later somehow extended to five years, to provide all the books for all the public libraries in Hawaii. This arrangement was made possible, in part, because the libraries in Hawaii are centrally controlled. A political alliance between the governor, the state librarian, and Baker & Taylor led to this controversial contract (an alliance with Dynix had a similar outcome in the libraries' "choice" of an automated system). As Broadfield noted 50 years ago, "Central control is generally used in the interest of the controllers" (page 40). In this case the interests were both financial and political, as the outsourcing of libraries was ballyhooed by the governor as a model for "reinventing" the whole state government.

As books began pouring into the Hawaiian libraries, it quickly became clear, to the frontline librarians at least, that B&T was clearing its shelves by unloading a lot of old, unwanted material that was unlikely to interest anyone, and including multiple copies of Newt Gingrich's mostly unread novel *1945*, copies that most likely would otherwise have been pulped, and plenty of paperback copies of the movie tie-in *Flipper*, which B&T selectors were sure would be of interest to Hawaiians, all at $20.94 a copy.

Baker & Taylor was unprepared for the reaction, thinking that librarians in Hawaii were only remotely connected to librarians on the mainland. Little did they realize that the internet had changed all that. They didn't realize that a library science student in Texas, Pat Wallace, could and would lead a challenge to B&T's colonization of Hawaiian libraries.

Pat Wallace quickly found allies through the internet, including Charles Willett, Sandy Berman, Chris Dodge, and myself. Again the internet made it possible to publicize what was happening in Hawaii quickly, so that librarians around the country were able to read and react in a matter of months, rather than years. The internet became a zone of virtual freedom, a method for leveraging enormous amounts of information rapidly.

At the same time, encouraged by the response from the mainland, the Hawaiian librarians were able to challenge the state librarian and the governor, continuing to gather and disseminate information over the internet, showing how the B&T contract was shortchanging their libraries. The library administrators tried, too late, to impose a gag order on the librarians. But by this time the electronic net was established, and two or three people were able to both coordinate the flow of information among librarians in Hawaii and maintain the flow of information to the mainland.

Ultimately, the librarians in Hawaii, bolstered by the support of mainland librarians, were able to generate a lot of criticism about the B&T outsourcing deal. This led to an inquiry from the state government, spearheaded by Senator Tam. Eventually, after hearings, the Hawaii legislature voted to outlaw this form of outsourcing. The state librarian was forced into the position of repudiating the contract he had earlier helped to write. Now both sides are suing each other, and it may be years before the dust clears.

In spite of this scandal, book vendors and library administrators will continue to push outsourcing as the wave of the future. In this sense, they are following a trend that, at least in the business world, had already come and gone. In the business world, managers have already experienced the myriad problems that come from outsourcing, and many are already advocating more employee participation in place of centralized control and outsourcing. Managers have found, much to their surprise, that employee loyalty does have value and rewards for the company far beyond what can be measured in the nickels and dimes saved by outsourcing contracts.

The real tragedy of library outsourcing is the realization of just how many library administrators and library school faculty are willing to sell out their profession by pushing outsourcing (and other similar schemes) just in order to gain a short-term personal advantage in their own careers. Their betrayal of the profession, and of library patrons, quickly followed their betrayal of themselves and their own values.

7. But What Is a Library For?

During Broadfield's lifetime there were various people who predicted that public libraries would be taken over by educational institutions and that they would be converted over to a wholly educational function. Broadfield viewed this possibility with considerable horror, saying:

> The school typically emphasizes standardization and necessarily must regiment when classes, curriculums, credits and school terms are involved. But the school is weak on adaptation to individual needs, interests and talents when these diverge far from the norm [page 44].

Clearly, Broadfield felt that libraries were for the growth and enlightenment of the individual, not the education or social control of the great masses of people who visit the library for their personal entertainment or to get simple information. To a large extent, patrons need to be treated as individuals with widely varied needs. They are not a "mass"; they are not in groups whose needs can be generalized, nor should their reading interests be massaged into pigeonholes by the librarian.

People are different, and they experience things in different ways, often ways we would find rather difficult to understand. This tends to make reference service a very hit-and-miss enterprise. Just ask anyone who does reference in a patent library, where you have to help patrons without really knowing very much about what they are looking for (as they don't want to tell you). Or try doing reference in an art or music library, where patrons often have only a vague generalized idea of what they are looking for.

I tend to agree, wholeheartedly, with Broadfield's views on education. Putting libraries into the role of educators is a very limiting one, especially since we still have a very vague understanding of what constitutes education and how we know when someone has got it.

For example, I attended a rural high school in Cave City, Arkansas, where I graduated a remarkable seventh in my class (of 47 seniors). Luckily, the authors of the SAT and ACT exams had a better appreciation of my abilities than my teachers did, and I was able to get a very good scholarship to Lyon College, a liberal arts school in the Ozark foothills, and eventually graduated cum laude. Later on I got masters' degrees at the University of Arkansas–Fayetteville and the University of Wisconsin-Madison. On the other hand, at the same time I was graduating seventh out of 47 in my high school class, a student who graduated well ahead of me barely managed to score in the double digits on her ACT exam. Some years later she became a schoolteacher, and later a school superintendent (which either says something about the ACT or something about school superintendents). Anyway, the point here is that different educational measures often give wildly different results. So please consider this still another argument against using a rigid system of educational measurement and placement like the ones used extensively in Europe and Japan.

It is equally difficult to "measure" library service, and it's hard to know when we have actually answered a question or only further confused the patron. In fact, the information needs of library patrons vary widely, just as their aesthetic tastes differ. And, as James McNeil Whistler pointed out in his famous lecture *Ten o'Clock*, it is useless and counterproductive to try to induce people into liking art that they just really don't enjoy. It's like teaching pigs to whistle. People like what they like, and we must allow that even professional wrestling may have some redeeming social value that we simply, as yet, don't quite understand.

To put a less than subtle point on this issue, let me tell you about a tourist trap in Wisconsin called the House on the Rock. Several years ago my wife and I were driving through southwest Wisconsin and decided to visit the famous House on the Rock "tourist attraction" near Spring Green. This place is a house constructed on and around a towering spire of rock, and built so that it wraps around to become almost a part of the rock. It is, in its own right, an interesting piece of architecture.

As we walked through the house, we noted the weird collection of "museum pieces"—a strange menagerie of bad art collected from all over the world and spread willy-nilly throughout the house. In small doses this collection of so-called art seemed interesting, in a peculiar sort of way, even though these objects didn't really fit in very well with the design of the house, which had been inspired to some extent by Frank Lloyd Wright (who had lived nearby and been an acquaintance of the man who had originally designed and built this house).

After going through the house, we saw that, included in the price of admission, was the chance to go through the art museum—a series of warehouse-like buildings nearby. As we started walking through the museum, we saw the same strange and bizarre art works, again collected and displayed in a willy-nilly fashion, with dark wooden African masks and sculpture sitting next to bright pastels, pink feathers and crystal glassware. The effect was, at first, amusing. But soon it became uncomfortable, as the garish art began to take its toll on our nervous systems.

Pretty soon we were walking quickly through the displays, trying not to look too closely at the Victorian/Baroque/Art Deco/Modern/African/Asian/Siberian Eskimo/etc./etc. objets d'art in the displays. The only obvious criteria used by the collectors was that each item on display had to exhibit some peculiar feature that sent it careening over the edge from what might have been an odd conversation piece into the category of *really* bad art. Soon we were nearly running, pushing past people while trying desperately to get out of the building. And then we saw It. Advertised as "The World's Largest Ferris Wheel," it was immense and covered with many thousands of brightly colored lights, but contained within the building so that you had no choice but to go past it at close quarters. Try to imagine attending a Polish wedding on LSD and you might come close to understanding what it was like standing in proximity to It.

We desperately looked for an exit, but each door was set with an alarm and was clearly marked FOR EMERGENCIES ONLY. And how do you explain to someone that you have an aesthetic emergency? We finally decided to suffer through the last displays and hoped that a couple of aspirin and a nap would heal the psychic wounds.

Eventually we made our way out of the museum and out to our car. As we drove down the road, we were both still a little woozy from the experience. But a few minutes on the road, surrounded by green grass and a blue sky, soon provided relief from the psychological mugging we had received. And then we saw a sign for Taliesin.

Little known outside of Wisconsin, Taliesin is a school of architecture established by Frank Lloyd Wright some years ago. Wright was a Wisconsin native and owned some land near Spring Green. The Taliesin school allows visitors to tour its complex of buildings, see some of the designs, and look through the library, which includes models of many buildings designed by Wright.

Never having visited Taliesin before, and still reeling from our visit to the House on the Rock, we were unsure about stopping. But luckily we decided to chance it. As it turns out, Taliesin was something quite different from our last stop. The collection of buildings, done in the familiar Wright style, convey a sense of grace to the whole area. Some of the buildings were in need of repair, and there were few visitors that day, but it was still a world away from the tourist trap just down the road.

It is impossible to really convey the almost religious aura that surrounds Taliesin. This place conveys a reality, perhaps not unlike the feeling you might get while visiting a medieval abbey, or perhaps a cathedral. There is a sense of space, as a thing of beauty unto itself. Taliesin is a monument to an ideal of beauty and design, and so it seemed quite out of place when compared to the rest of the world, or at least to the places that lie just outside it.

On the way back to Madison, we talked about why so few people were visiting Taliesin, compared with the thousands who poured into the House on the Rock. My wife had just recently finished Ayn Rand's *The Fountainhead*, and she described for me Rand's theory of art. Rand evidently believed that any time something beautiful and honest was created, the forces of mediocrity try to destroy it. And if it cannot be destroyed, then these forces build some attraction near it, to draw attention away from it, so that people will pass it by. Applied to Taliesin, this theory seems to make sense.

Similarly, a few weeks ago we visited Eureka Springs, Arkansas — a small resort town that had, years ago, been a health resort and artists' colony. Today the town is really, for the most part, a tourist trap, with the hideous Christ of the Ozarks placed as the lure to draw tourists into the gaping maw of the trap. While driving through town, we saw a sign for Pivot Rock, a natural wonder that had been mentioned years ago in Ripley's Believe-It-or-Not series. This time we decided to travel down the back roads to see the rock, perhaps in spite of Mr. Ripley's endorsement, and thereby testing Ayn Rand's theory of art.

After driving several miles of narrow back road, and with at least one false turn with a retracing of our route, we came to the small building that leads into the Pivot Rock park. As it turns out, the park includes a natural bridge and a series of strange cliffs, including Pivot Rock and several other naturally carved rocks, but of the nonpivoting variety. Actually, the place was really very impressive, and a true contrast to the ugly, fatuous messiah-in-concrete that stood on the mountain on the other side of town. We enjoyed the park, arriving just as a morning rain had ended, the flintstone gleaming from the moisture. But soon we were on the road again.

A few minutes later (and against my better judgment) we stopped to visit an old Victorian house, called the Queen Anne Mansion, which was located right on the main highway in Eureka Springs. Built in 1889, the house was of an ornate Victorian design, but none of the original furnishings were still around when the current owners bought it in 1984. So, unfortunately, the owners "traveled extensively to look for exceptional pieces of various styles." As you can imagine, this phrase is probably the greatest understatement of all time. In fact, the owners accumulated a garish collection of furniture that would have been right at home in the House on the Rock.

There are, of course, thousands of tourist traps pretty much like this one all over the United States; and they seem to cater directly to people who have a taste for really bad art. In my case, I live just a few minutes away from the Precious Moments Chapel in Carthage, Missouri, and so I have a constant reminder, near at hand, of a particularly bad example of artistic kitsch.

In my role as Collection Development librarian, I am often given books of questionable artistic taste, published by a variety of publishers. I try to add them to the collection, whenever they look like they might be useful. Again, as much as I may disagree with some of their taste in art, the library should be a place of inclusion, rather than exclusion.

8. But What Does This Have to Do with Libraries?

The fact is, what happens in architecture also happens in book publishing. We saw, with the House on the Rock and Taliesin, an example of how corporate culture creates elaborate "fakes" that are intended to distract people from "The Real Thing," as they say (un-ironically) in Coke commercials. People, who might really benefit from visiting Taliesin and seeing the work of Frank Lloyd Wright and his followers, instead see the poor imitation of Wright's style, along with a museum of garish bric-a-brac.

I would not go to the lengths suggested by Ayn Rand and claim that there is a conspiracy going on. The people who made the House on the Rock what it is today were simply exploiting what had already existed; they took advantage of the situation and probably thought the addition of the ugly art "museum" was a good idea. The Rock's proximity to Taliesin might simply be due to a chain of historical events rather than a conspiracy. It would be more accurate to say that many people, like the creator of the House on the Rock, are aesthetically paralyzed and therefore unable to distinguish "the weird" from "the beautiful." Much like people who buy collector's plates, they have money, but they have no artistic sense.

This situation carries over into publishing. At any given time there are thousands of manuscripts circulating through the publishing houses of New York on any given topic you can imagine. Some of these manuscripts represent the work of genuinely talented writers, and many of these manuscripts are the work of lousy hacks. But most are the work of mediocrities.

Publishing houses are naturally inclined to publish the work of mediocrities. Most of these books are fairly interesting and they tend to be written in an easy style that is readily comprehended by the average high school graduate. More important, none of them are likely to suggest ideas that might challenge the existing status quo, including the power relationships that are important to the media conglomerates that own the publishing houses. And so the books published by the big publishers in New York tend to be those that, although they raise important issues, usually suggest as "remedies" actions that are not likely to be effective.

A good example of this type of book is David C. Korten's *When Corporations Rule the World*. Although the title might suggest a more radical view than you might expect, in reality the book does little more than raise questions. The answers it suggests would do little to change the status quo. To put it another way, Korten's book is an excellent analysis of what is wrong, but it does a lousy job of suggesting ways to fix the problem. It encourages cynicism, and that's about it. Similarly, Hendrick Smith's *Rethinking America* is a book with a lot of good ideas. Smith believes that power-sharing in organizations is the trend of the future and suggests various ways this can be accomplished. Unfortunately these ideas are only likely to be adopted by organizations that are already in serious trouble. A corporation with a healthy bottom-line rarely considers sharing power with workers.

A more dubious book is Michael Cosgrove's *The Cost of Winning:*

Global Development Policies and Broken Social Contracts. Again, the author comes up with an excellent analysis of the problem, but the solutions he offers do little to remedy the situation. For example, Cosgrove thinks that simply moving Congress out of Washington, D.C., will break the cycle of corruption that exists in the way Congress does business. However, he does nothing to address the fact that congressmen are heavily dependent on money from lobbyists and special interest groups.

Similarly, after the recent scandal in which the Clinton administration was accused of turning the White House into a virtual bed and breakfast for fundraising, there was a (briefly) renewed call for public financing of elections. As usual, this latest call for reform was short-lived. After all, a successful movement for public financing would need the support of the media. And since the media derive enormous amounts of money and power from the way things are now, they are unlikely to support a call for public funding. For the short term, at least, we will have to settle for having, as Will Rogers once said, "the best government money can buy."

Instead of focusing attention on reforms that might actually have an impact, the media focuses attention on phony reforms that, although they may have a populist angle, really would only serve to further the power of the media. For example, we hear a steady drumbeat of support these days for "term limits" but few people realize that this so-called "reform" would only further the interests of the media and their allies. As it stands now, congressmen are heavily dependent on big contributions from corporations and special interests. Eventually, however, once a politician has been re-elected several times, he or she tends to feel safe from potential challengers. Look at how many times people have tried (and failed) to "knock off" Senator Jesse Helms. Personally, I'm no great fan of Jesse Helms or any of the other congressmen who have been in office for decades. Yet I'd rather have an established politician in office, who might — assuming the notion struck him — have the wherewithal to vote his conscience rather than his pocketbook. I would, as a general rule, rather have a congressman who was not completely dependent on big contributors (meaning corporations and special interests) than a congressman who always has his eye on the next campaign or on his future career as a lobbyist. A senator who knows that he or she can serve only two terms, because of term limits, will end up spending an inordinate amount of time currying favor with the corporate powers-that-be. His real interest will be his future job as a consultant or lobbyist, not the public interest.

The media, on the other hand, would rather have congressmen who are more dependent on "good press" and more subservient to the monied interests in Washington. And that is why there is so much support for term limits. It is a phony reform, like the "flat-tax" reform, that will only serve to promote the interests of the wealthy and the media conglomerates they control. That is why they "push" this so-called reform so much.

In the library world we have to deal with similar phony reforms. For example, John Berry wrote an editorial in *Library Journal* entitled "Senator McCain's Phony 'Protection'" in which Berry criticizes efforts to link internet filters to the special E-rate subsidies for libraries. Berry correctly points out that pedophiles typically use e-mail to approach children, not websites, and that Senator McCain's reform does not address that problem at all. It does let Senator McCain take a phony "stand" against pornography and pedophiles, so it is sure to get plenty of votes in Congress.

Similarly, the Congress and the media have gone after the Clinton administration for taking contributions from "foreign" corporations for his 1996 presidential campaign. The political pundits are all so angry that they are fit to be tied. There is a lot of talk of more "campaign finance reform" in Washington, but this is also a fake reform. The problem is that political campaigns are driven by political contributions. Does it really matter whether Clinton is owned by Rupert Murdoch or Gallo Wine? Is there really a difference between being bought by the Japanese and being bought by the Chinese? Whether the contributors are "foreign" or "domestic" is of little importance to most of us, and pretending that "foreign" contributions are somehow more corrupting than contributions from American corporations seems to be naive in the extreme. But this idea is currently being promoted in the media, so it must be right.

The publishing industry is probably the most important part of our current media empires. They have the most influence on the future, through the publication of textbooks. They have the most control of the past, through publishing history books. And the present, that is pretty well sewn up through magazines and the electronic media. Very little in the way of alternative materials finds its way into print, and even less finds its way into bookstores or libraries. The focus of the media is on the latest scandal or the latest celebrity biography, not on the vital issues that confront our generation.

The books that are published by the big New York publishers tend to encourage cynicism about politics and politicians. This, too, serves the interest of the media, as they do not want to encourage political activism. The media are quite happy with things as they are. This country has a large body of people who are disaffected. They are convinced that politics is corrupt, and so they usually don't bother to vote, let alone get involved in political campaigns. The people who do vote are usually those citizens who are easily manipulated by the media. Any attempt to change this situation is usually micro-analyzed and dissected by the press, as for example the way the Ross Perot campaign was created and then demolished by the media.

Perot was created by the media largely to distract people from more serious reform movements. But when it looked like Perot might actually win, then the media had to destroy him. I seem to recall that this premise is used in the political films *All the King's Men* and *Mr. Smith Goes to Washington*, so this is hardly a new idea. I guess you could say that, whether you are talking about Ross Perot, the House on the Rock, or Camelot, there are plenty of popular diversions out there, created to keep people from seeing Taliesin, or whatever true vision is hidden in the media vacuum, removed from popular view. The goal of the librarian is to collect material, not just on the popular diversions, but to actively search for alternative materials and unpopular ideas that may be purposely ignored or even actively suppressed by the media.

It may be necessary to do some serious digging to figure out what is real and what is phony. One of the best indicators of a phony issue or a phony reform is how much press it gets. One of the most cynical and vicious "reforms" to be promoted in the press is the idea of privatizing the social security system. A whole army of economists and political pundits have come forward, claiming to want to "save" social security. They claim that the best way to do this is for individuals to have personal accounts and invest their social security contributions in the stock market. Since the stock market has been growing rapidly in recent years, this seems like a safe bet. Or is it?

In fact, the stock market has in recent years been artificially inflated by the retirement investments of the baby boom generation, and when the majority of baby boomers retire there will be an enormous sucking sound and a solid downward pressure on the value of stocks. It is virtually impossible to avoid a major collapse of stock values, once the baby boomers start selling their stocks and using the money to fund their retirements (see, for example, Kinsella).

By creating a privatized social security system, Wall Street hopes to, at least temporarily, prevent the collapse of stock prices. A large influx of new cash from young workers would probably help bolster the stock market, but at what price? Eventually, the people who have moved to a "privatized" retirement program will be hit with a falling stock market and a decline in the value of their retirement portfolios. Many people following in the wake of the boomers will face a lower standard of living and a meager retirement. We may even see scenes, like those in Russia today, where grandmothers stand on street corners selling pencils in order to supplement an almost nonexistent pension.

It's hard to imagine a more cynically motivated "reform." In fact, this reform surpasses in pure greed the so-called reform of the savings and loan system in the 1980s. And it will require an even more massive bailout from public funds. Yet virtually no one in the media points out these facts, a sure sign that the corporate media in this country are dominated by corporate interests devoted to misinformation and misdirection (see, for example, the April 27, 1998, issue of *Newsweek*, including the sickening ad-itorial by George Will, the reigning Prince of Intellectual Darkness). It is for this reason that librarians *must* search more diligently for alternative viewpoints to include in library collections.

9. *The Library of the Future—Its Goals.*

> The risk of tyranny cannot be eliminated by even the most carefully worked out constitutional methods. A vigorous intellectual life sustained by ample provision of books is more effective. Nor can insidious orthodoxies be avoided by even the strongest tradition of liberty: indeed when liberty has become a tradition it is too late to hope for its preservation [Broadfield, page 51].

Assume for a moment that libraries are a battleground for ideas. The question then becomes: Does one side or the other have an unfair advantage?

If you ask the combatants, from the Right and the Left, this question is usually answered: "Sure! The other side has all the advantages."

So we need to go to another source in evaluating how well each side is doing in the culture war.

Obviously, there are winners and losers in the culture war. Certainly the participants have advantages and disadvantages in putting forth their army of materials, and their positions shift over time. During the Red Scare in the 1950s, few people felt that the library should have any materials at all that were pro-communist. During the following decades, that attitude shifted somewhat, so that today most libraries have a few "radical" materials. But even so there is still a strong, almost irresistible desire by partisans on both the left and right, not just to promote their own views, which we would tend to encourage, but also to censor the other side's views. And it is these attempts at censorship that we need to resist.

More and more frequently, "minority" religious groups go into libraries and vandalize materials critical of their sect. This kind of vandalism used to be limited to puritanical patrons who would cut out "dirty" pictures from books or magazines. In one case I recall, a patron regularly checked out books and used a black marker to mark out "dirty" words. I presume we can still call them "patrons" even when they come into the library in order to deface or damage the collection. You should consider yourself lucky if this behavior is limited to the patrons and does not occur within the library staff, as I know of one library where a staff member regularly defaced pro-choice material and stuffed the pamphlet file with pro-life brochures. This same staff member was a frequent witness to the "liberal bias" of the other librarians whenever a local group wanted to challenge library materials. I would humbly suggest that she was entitled to her opinions, such as they were, but defacing library materials was going a bit too far! Perhaps we need a Geneva Convention for libraries, or at least some agreement that the combatants should not set fire to the library in order to make a point. They may set fire to themselves as long as they stand well away from the stacks.

In another case, I met a school librarian here in Kansas who, when the *Sports Illustrated* swimsuit issue arrives each year, takes a huge property stamp and stamps/smears ink all over the bikini photos. This kind of "censorship" is probably the most common form found in libraries. All too often, librarians use their own policies and procedures to suppress things they don't like. On the other hand, librarians have also been known to like some library materials a bit too much. When my wife worked part-time for a county library in Wisconsin, the library purchased a copy of *Looking Good*, a guide to "style" for men, which contained dozens of pictures of good-looking male models. By the time this book finally made it out of the technical services area, the ILL area, the circulation area (and so on), and onto the new book shelf, the book was worn out and the library had to order a new copy!

At the library I sometimes hear complaints from the workers in technical services when we buy books that include photos of nude women. But, when we buy books with nude men, usually all I hear are giggles. And the professional librarians usually aren't much help when it comes to defending "controversial" material. When several of the older civil service staff members complained about Thomas Waugh's *Hard to Imagine*, a book on the history of gay male erotica, a librarian came to my defense by saying that she didn't see anything in the book that she hadn't seen before. A few years earlier, when the purchase of a book on lesbian photography was questioned by a staff member, another librarian, trying to be helpful, said, "I've seen worse than that!"

As a collection development librarian, I welcome gift books into the library, and that does mean gifts from all sides, even the pro-life stuff with the gross pictures. Personally, I prefer a book written by a person who carries his prejudices on his sleeve over the books with a hidden agenda. For this reason, I welcome book catalogs from Prometheus Books, the Cato Institute, and similar organizations, since I don't have to wonder about what hidden agenda is being promoted. The publishers' biases are clearly visible and presented in a forthright manner. I prefer dealing with a publisher who has an obvious political or ethical viewpoint to promote and who is not just in it for the money.

I like to keep my prejudices out in front of me, so I can keep an eye on them. I also like to believe that I've come by my prejudices honestly, and I like to examine my preconceptions fairly often, just to make sure they are still viable. I want to say too that our library owned a copy of the antigovernment novel *The Turner Diaries* back before it became fashionable or politically incorrect. Our copy has, since then, been stolen, but that is typical with antigovernment books — some of our dogmatically antigovernment patrons just hate the hassle of dealing with the lazy, overpaid, government employees in our circulation department. It's just easier to steal the book.

There are lots of books I like, but books are like people, and there are plenty of books that are hard to like. Personally, I find textbooks to be in this category. Mostly, they are poorly written and tend to gloss over serious issues, *Reader's Digest*-like, in order to pounce on the obvious. They tend to skirt or even ignore important issues (in order to avoid controversy) which short-changes the readers who rely on them for information. At the other extreme, there are books that I especially like, including a good deal of nonfiction. Some books, like Michael Lind's *The Next American Nation*, are intelligent and informative. There are other books that are simply a pleasure to read, like Jacques Lacarriere's *The Gnostics*, and serve to both inform and delight.

One thing that a collection development librarian should learn fairly quickly is how to judge various publishers by what they produce. There are some publishers who can be relied on to produce a good book, day in and day out, because they have a commitment to producing literature that is clearly and cogently written. For example, if I want a book on philosophy or religion, I can turn to Open Court, HarperCollins, or Prometheus. If I want a book on critical theory, I can turn to one of several university presses including Oxford, Cambridge, Chicago and several others. Even in the subject area of New Age books, which is notorious for bad writing, you can turn to Shambhala or Element for a good read. These are, of course, my own personal opinions and other librarians may have different views and different preferences — at least I hope they do.

Textbooks are the mainstays of our cherished myths, and so they are one of the main obstacles to getting a good education in this country. If you doubt this, simply read a description of the Civil War in any high school textbook, and then read any good history of the Civil War. The difference in the quality of both the writing and the information should be obvious. Most students would be better off reading books from the library than getting their information from textbooks.

As a teacher of college freshman-level English, I spent a great deal of time trying to get students to ignore "the rules" they were taught in their high school English classes. These rules were invented as shortcuts, but in many cases they became handicaps that did more to inhibit students than help. Students need to learn grammar and composition, not just memorize a lot of rules. The best book for this purpose is Claude Faulkner's *Writing Good Sentences*, since it takes a natural language approach to grammar and sentence construction. After all, what is the point of trying to teach students a lot of rules about where commas go, if the students don't really have a working knowledge of English grammar? But instead of teaching grammar as a natural function, schools concentrate on tree diagramming (which is almost worthless) and transformational grammar (which is worse than useless), ignoring the natural structure of English.

Some years ago I was told to use a student evaluation form in the English classes I was teaching. The form was standardized, allowing the students to rank my teaching from 1 to 5 in different areas. One question asked them to rank "the teacher's ability to make complex ideas simple." But I wasn't really sure how I would want them to answer this question. After all, if an idea is complex, can it be reduced to a simple idea? This seems to be the main premise of modern textbooks, that the complex can be reduced to simplicity, if only it is presented in the right way. This assumption appears to lie behind most theories of media and education today, which explains a lot about what is wrong with our schools and with television — two of the main influences on our children. Complex ideas exist, and they cannot be reduced or simplified for popular consumption without causing confusion. This confusion is the source of our "common opinions" on all sorts of issues — opinions that are usually dead wrong.

A. Broadfield was well aware of the problem of these "mass beliefs" and how they are promoted, especially in textbooks. In particular he quoted a literature textbook that states, "It is not certain that Henry James belongs to American literature for he was critical of America and admired Europe." The built-in biases of textbooks are sometimes (as in this case) laughable, but I suspect that the poor writing in textbooks is as much responsible as any other single cause for the high numbers of students who drop out of high school. The students may not "know" that these textbooks are being dumbed-down, but they do realize that somehow they are being culturally short-changed.

To put it another way, both textbooks and teachers tend to state the obvious as if it were a new idea. For example, last week I was walking through a school building, following behind two teachers who were taking a refresher course in geography. They had just finished a pop-quiz and I overheard one teacher say to the other: "I could have answered that last question if I'd known that 'Rio' meant river and 'Grande' meant large." I nodded my head in agreement. Yes, that is true. And that is what is wrong about the way we teach most subjects in school. We teach in order to prepare our students to take some multiple-choice exam, like the SAT or the ACT. We assume that knowing the data is the same as understanding. Somehow, the essence of the thing keeps escaping us — over and over again.

We are well aware of the fact, too, that Americans have a very different political culture from people in other countries. Or, as Broadfield so politely put it, "The American has a fairly good idea of his individual requirements and is not docile where his interests are concerned" (page 52). There is a natural tendency for Americans, as noted by Broadfield and many, many other writers throughout our history, to resist regimentation. Our society and our culture usually reflect these tendencies. Our books, with the exception of textbooks, also tend to reflect an American obsession with individualism. Many other societies do not share this tendency, and it is reflected in their history, their politics, and their books. For example, read Daikichi Irokawa's history *The Age of Hirohito*. This book reads like it was written by a textbook committee; yet, to judge by its press, evidently the Japanese consider this book to be quite entertaining. One might wonder if the problem was with the translator, but reading the text you can see how the author very carefully and precisely avoids saying anything that might cause offense.

Americans, on the other hand, seem to work constantly to find new ways to offend. Stand-up comics have, in recent years, been trying to perfect offensiveness as if it were a fine art. And where else in the world would there be so much interest in books describing techniques for getting "revenge" against those who have offended you? There are dozens of titles in print, including *The Black Book of Revenge* and *Gaslighting: How to Drive Your Enemies Crazy*. There is a reaction against this, too, with dozens of books being published on the need for "civility" in public affairs. Personally, I would rather deal with someone like the person described by Herman Melville as "a good hater." A good hater is easily identified and avoided. But they are unlike the devious sorts out there, the men and women with a "lean and hungry look" who will stab you in the back the first chance they get.

This is part of why the overt racism directed at blacks in the South was fairly easily uprooted, and this was accomplished in this country in a single generation. The hidden racism, directed at blacks, Jews, and other minorities is much harder to deal with. And so I think most of us are much happier dealing with a Governor Faubus, standing in the schoolhouse door, than the sneaking bigot who hides his malice, "who smiles and smiles, and yet is still a villain."

For the librarian, the best policy is to make common cause with those people in the community who share your interests. After all, why would you trust someone whom you are unsure of, when you can rely more firmly on those who share a common (self) interest in promoting libraries and civil liberties? Some people will suggest that people in the community can "transcend" their own interests and make sacrifices that will benefit your library. This may be true, but you are better off relying on those who need you than placing any great faith in those who may claim they want to help you. As Broadfield notes, university libraries in England, the United States, and the Soviet Union were able to do their part in helping to overthrow the Nazi regime in Germany. But they did not do it by trying to transcend their national interests. American universities worked to overthrow Hitler because "Americans universities are dedicated to the American way of life" (page 55), and they were determined to support the Allied cause in defeating Fascism. A pretended common interest is not to be relied on, except when there is no other option at hand.

Similarly, a librarian who is confronted with a censorship challenge is probably wiser to rely on those elements in the community who have a vested interest in preserving civil liberties, particularly bookstores and the local media, rather than seeking help too far afield. What happens when a librarian stands alone, trying to put "Truth" ahead of the public interest? Usually, the local community leaders get out the tar and feathers, and they are at the head of the crowd that runs you out of town on a rail. Community leaders usually place a high value on conformity. After all, that is the foundation stone upon which they have built their community.

Sometimes the need for conformity can be used to your advantage. That is why it is important for a public librarian to be involved with local clubs and churches, and that is why a university librarian should take pains to be involved, as much as possible, in the governance of the university. It is, for example, instructive to look at the career of Ervin Szabo, who served for some years as the director of the library of Budapest. Szabo was very active, politically, yet managed to maintain his position through his reputation for integrity. He never lost sight of the fact that his primary purpose was to serve the people in his community. And his political actions were derived naturally from that goal. In this way Szabo is not far different from Ben Franklin and other political leaders.

If a librarian is perceived as being an integral part of the local community, then it will be much easier to withstand challenges to so-called controversial materials in the library. Indeed, it is easier to paint the censor as an "outsider" or "interloper" or "fanatic" when the librarian is already seen and accepted as an insider. This is especially important when trying to defend books like Jane Caputi's *The Age of Sex Crime* or Robin Baker's *Sperm Wars*, which are likely to be attacked by both liberals and conservatives. These are both powerful books, but they have little in the way of a built-in constituency, and so their preservation as part of the collection may depend heavily on the reputation for good judgment and fair play of the library staff.

The most formidable enemy of the librarian is intolerance, and intolerance is most often the product of ignorance, "which libraries seek to remove by the spread of knowledge, pleasant and unpleasant, approved and disapproved, useful and useless" (page 70). Broadfield further states that intolerant societies deprive people of the ability to be tolerant in three ways: first, by depriving people of a sense of responsibility; second, by weakening their control over their own selves; and third, by restricting access to materials that might serve to make people more tolerant.

In order to promote tolerance, the librarian needs to make common cause with those people and institutions outside the library who can be relied on to resist censorship efforts. But it doesn't end there. The goal of the librarian should include working to help people develop a sense of responsibility for their own actions. This also means helping people to gain a sense of control over their own lives, since this is a necessary step toward self-sufficiency. The librarian should collect materials that support these efforts and develop library policies and programs that further these goals. These efforts all contribute to the promotion of tolerance in the community.

10. Tolerant or Impartial?

A. Broadfield rightly notes that the goal of the library should be to create a place where opinions may be freely distributed. Thus librarians' duties should include resisting the efforts of censors to interfere with the dissemination of unpopular ideas. The library should not become a reflection of the librarian's values, carrying only the materials that reflect his or her opinions. Rather the library should house a variety of opinions "pleasant and unpleasant" (page 70).

All the views that we now accept as scientific fact began as simply opinions, although some were more popular than others. But popularity does not change an opinion into a fact. At one time, virtually everyone on earth agreed that the earth was flat and that the sun went around the earth. Many centuries passed before these opinions were finally eradicated (if they have, in fact, been eradicated — or are they, like smallpox, going to return to haunt us later?). Public opinion moves of its own weight, like a snowball going down a hillside, building up speed and size until it overwhelms everything in front of it. The great mass of books and magazines in the library will reflect popular ideas and common notions. This is inevitable. So our real goal is to actively search for and acquire those ideas that are unpopular and uncommon, for they are as likely to be correct as the popular ideas. Courage is needed in order to build a diverse collection.

Unfortunately, many librarians believe that the collection should be socially homogenous. Like the right-wing pundits who believe that all Americans share a "common culture" or a common set of values, their libraries tend to reflect a middle-class set of values and prejudices. Historically, libraries are a creation of the middle class. But that does not mean that they should necessarily reflect middle-class values in the material they collect. We are under an obligation to serve our communities, but that also means that we should educate and inform our patrons about other cultures and other values.

We may strive to be impartial, but that is not a common quality among human beings, and librarians are still, for the most part, human beings with human failings. We can, in some cases, neglect to acquire material that is obviously false or poorly conceived. For example, I once read a newspaper called *Wisconsin Report*, published by a one-man operation in the hinterlands of that state. In a front page article, the publisher/author claimed that the United States lost a nuclear war with Russia that was fought on the moon. In retaliation, the U.S. forces captured a Russian nuclear missile base in Guyana, discovered by an American "agent" named Jim Jones.

Yes, this was shortly after the Jonestown tragedy, where hundreds of Americans committed suicide under the orders of cult leader Jim Jones. The author of this article, Dr. Peter Beter (I'm *not* making this up!), decided that the metal canisters brought back from Guyana, which the U.S. government claims contained the bodies of suicide victims, were actually full of nuclear warheads we had captured from the Russians. This newspaper had several similar articles, including an exposé of secular humanist ideas hidden in a popular history textbook and an advertisement for non-cling baptismal gowns.

Needless to say, I don't think most libraries would have much need for a subscription to *Wisconsin Report*. Although the ideas in this paper are unpopular, I think it wouldn't be too much of a stretch to suggest that they are probably also dead wrong, given the publisher's lack of interest in the need for evidence before making wild accusations. If an article in this paper did prove to be true, it would be true in the same way that a broken watch is right twice a day. Libraries might accept a free subscription, for its entertainment value, but paying for a subscription would be unnecessary under even the most open collection policy.

At the same time, a librarian needs to avoid too rigorous a skepticism in these matters. Sometimes even the supermarket tabloids manage to get the story right, though perhaps more by accident than intention. When dealing with controversial issues, it is necessary for the library to provide a forum for all sides that might be true, whether or not the ideas are popular. Ultimately, the fate of truth lies not with the librarian, but with the discerning patron. And so we provide a variety of views and opinions in the hope that we might accidentally provide a little bit of truth in there, mixed up with the menagerie of opinions.

Just as freedom can be said to exist in the junctures or "gaps" between the powers of various institutions, both private and public, we can say that truth exists where the various ideologies of the right and left come together in battle. The ideologues do battle, like bull elephants, and in the course of battle a tusk is broken off and falls to the earth. This bit of ivory is truth, the detritus of the battle between ideologies. Or, to put it plainly, a library exists as a battleground between the forces of the left and right, and the library's role in this conflict is to reflect a variety of perspectives on controversial issues, including those views that do not fit comfortably into the pigeonholes of "left" and "right."

It is important that the library not be too closely identified with the "common interest" since that usually implies that the library is only another instrument of government, of which it is usually a part, and has no obligation beyond serving the interests of that government. In fact, the library should serve the public, including those who do not use the library and those who are too poor to pay taxes. We serve the public interest, perhaps only in an indirect way. But we still serve as an institution that promotes an inclusive view of society.

For this reason it is important for libraries to collect "alternative" materials, and especially materials that are published locally, including zines, comics, newsletters, and other "self-published" material. Even if these materials end up being segregated in a local history collection, they are still important to have available in the library. The quality of desk-top publishing has improved so much in recent years that these materials also deserve a good deal of consideration. Every library should have a procedure in place for collecting alternative library materials, and especially materials produced locally or regionally. There are many good resources for finding small press and "alternative" materials, including *Counterpoise*, *Alternative Press Review*, and many other publications which perform a review function.

11. Library "Partners" into the Future.

Book vendors, along with library automation vendors, like to talk, at least in their advertising, about a "partnership" between libraries and vendors. Personally, I like to think of the relationship between vendors and libraries in this way too, since I've never known of a partnership where one partner didn't have his hand firmly implanted in the pockets of the other partner. So, from this point of view, you could see our relationship with vendors as a partnership of sorts.

Generally, in my experience, I've found book vendors to be both honest and reliable. But we should not deceive ourselves into believing that they come by these qualities naturally. In fact, it is largely the market forces of competition that keep these guys honest. There are, of course, a few rogue elephants in this herd, but on the whole book vendors are an honest and reliable sort, especially the smaller independent organizations.

There is, however, a trend that has carried over from the business world and which is likely to cause a great deal of trouble for libraries in the future. It is the merger of companies into larger and larger conglomerates. Just recently the Federal Trade Commission approved the merger of Boeing and McDonnell-Douglas into one huge aerospace company. Supposedly, these companies needed to merge in order to be competitive internationally. In fact, both Boeing and McDonnell-Douglas are huge, dinosaur-like creatures, stumbling around in the swamp and trying to avoid the smaller mammals that are destined someday to replace them. The implication of the media is that these two large, ungainly creatures are somehow going to become more efficient as a result of this merger. In fact, they are probably going to become even more awkward and lazy, relying on their size alone to crush any competition from the upstart mammals.

This is the problem with monopolistic enterprises. They are mostly incompetent and rely on their size and on the advantages of monopoly to survive. If monopolies are more efficient, then why did the bill for my long-distance phone service go down after the government broke up AT&T? Perhaps they are more efficient only in soaking their customers.

When Ablex Publishing Corporation announced that it had been acquired by JAI Press, Inc., it was nice enough to send me a letter stating that "Many of the prices in *Books in Print* are no longer valid" and suggesting that I add $30 to the price listed in *Books in Print* in order to get an "estimate" of what their books would now cost. Such honesty is rare, and I appreciated the letter. Similarly, when Gale acquired the series *The Annual Register of World Events* from St. Martin's a few years ago, it virtually doubled the price on the new volumes. Frankly, anyone who suggests that such mergers, buyouts, or takeovers will cause an improvement in services or a decrease in prices — due to greater efficiency, elimination of duplication, etc.— is either lying or has started to believe the company's own PR (a sure sign of decrepitude or mental disease).

More recently, I received a letter from West Group, with a slogan written across the top; in big letters, it says "To Serve You Better." The letter goes on to explain that there has been a merger of Thomson Legal Publishing (which includes Bancroft Whitney and Lawyers Cooperative) and West Publishing. Somehow this is supposed to "serve" me better, but I doubt it. Now that these two publishers are no longer in competition, I expect my bills to go up for most of my legal services. This may correspond to better service, but I doubt it.

Most people don't understand the why and how of the merger mania that has run rampant in this country for over a decade now. I have an interesting angle on this, since my mother works in the banking industry. She works as the head teller and head of branch banks and is now a vice president (not as glorious as it sounds, believe me). In fact, during the last decade, the bank where she works has been bought and sold about five times. Each time the bank had a new owner, the new owners fired about a third of the staff, swapped out the employees' old stock for the new stock, and changed the bank's computer system.

The swapping of old stock for new has been a windfall, because the value of her retirement fund has doubled in value in five years. Of course, you can imagine how the big executives (with big retirement funds and big stock options) have benefited from these deals. The firing of a third of the staff has made a lot more work for the remaining employees, but it looks good on the profit and loss statement and it makes it easier to sell the bank again to the next company. The new computer systems have been a pain to learn, but now all the hard decisions are made by a computer analyst in

Little Rock, and no one in the bank has to worry anymore about being blamed for making a bad loan. In fact, just last month the computer decided to approve an unsecured loan to an 88-year-old man for a new prosthetic leg, to be paid back over 36 months. I can just imagine a bank employee being sent to the funeral home to repossess the leg after he passes on. Actually, I suspect that one of the local bank employees "massaged" this loan through the computer system just to help the old man get his leg — at least that's my theory.

In fact this bank is probably no more efficient or valuable a property than it was a decade ago, before the series of takeovers happened. The value of the bank stock has gone up for reasons totally unrelated to the value of the bank's assets or its potential income. The level of service is considerably less than it was a decade ago, given the decrease in the total number of employees, and a number of big customers are looking elsewhere with their accounts. The increase in value is all a paper increase. If the stock market falls, or crashes, the value of the stock will almost certainly go through the basement.

In reality, merger mania is a sign of weakness, not strength. A strong company could continue in business without needing a merger. Typically, a strong company is often taken over by a weak, but larger company that needs to "take over" the competition in order to survive. To this extent, William Dean Howells' novel *The Rise of Silas Lapham* is a pretty accurate depiction of how this process works. In the novel, Lapham realizes that his paint manufacturing company will eventually go out of business because a smaller competitor has access to raw materials at a much lower price. Lapham realizes that he can (1) try to force the other guys out of business through his larger size and control of markets, (2) try to buy them out, or (3) engineer a merger. Lapham, after considerable soul-searching, decides to try a merger. In Howells' novel, Silas Lapham is too ethical a person to simply crush his competition, which is why this book's happy ending may come off as too sentimental for most contemporary readers.

Most large publishers are now part of some conglomerate or other. HarperCollins, for example, is a small part of Rupert Murdoch's News Corporation, which owns Fox television, movie studios, cable television companies, *TV Guide*, and many other magazines and newspapers. These companies support each other and, in many subtle ways, compete with each other. It would be a mistake to see them all as part of some enormous beehive. That would be too simplistic a view. They are not really like the Borg, a race of cyborgs portrayed in *Star Trek: The Next Generation* as madly trying to conquer or "assimilate" the rest of the universe. I have heard some people suggest that the Borg are a parody of Microsoft

("Prepare to be assimilated!" they demand as they begin attacking the spaceship *Enterprise*), but the Borg could just as easily stand for any mega-corporation or corporate raider.

In reality, I believe that our society is coming, more and more, to resemble the society that already exists in Japan today. And for that reason, I would strongly recommend that everyone read Karel Van Wolferen's book *The Enigma of Japanese Power*, as a description of a modern dystopia. I believe that this is the direction we have begun moving — toward a "state-less" society, a society where large megacorporations have, in fact, complete control over both the government and the markets in which smaller entrepreneurs compete with each other (but not with the megacorporations, who use government regulation and market manipulation to derail any real competition). Some scholars, including William Warren Bartley, for whom I otherwise have a great deal of respect, tend to place Japan on a pedestal because of its successful rise from the ashes after the disaster of losing World War II. Bartley goes so far as to suggest that Hiroshima "shocked" the Japanese into adopting a pragmatic worldview, and that it was this new outlook that made their advances possible (*Unfathomed*, page 289). A more realistic assumption would be that Japan successfully manipulated the markets, much as Germany did in the 1930s, to create an industrial empire, and this was done at the expense of both the Japanese people and most of Asia.

We are, at the end of the 20th century, moving into a new era that I find disturbing. Our society is developing in ways that few could have anticipated a decade ago, and not all of the developments are good. On the whole, technology has provided many positive benefits, but the over-all slide into authoritarianism in both our political and economic institutions is still very real. And that is why I value the insights of A. Broadfield's book. There are many libertarians working in librarianship today, or at least librarians who subscribe to the anticensorship aspects of libertarianism. As librarians we have the power to look for and exploit small areas of freedom in an unfree world. This is the most important mission of libraries going into the 21st century.

REFERENCES

Bak, Janos M., ed. *Liberty and Socialism: Writings of Libertarian Socialists in Hungary, 1884–1919*. Savage, MD: Rowman & Littlefield, 1991.

Baker, Robin. *Sperm Wars: The Science of Sex*. New York: Basic, 1996.

Bakunin, Michael. *God and the State*. New York: Dover, 1970.

Balmary, Marie. *Psychoanalyzing Psychoanalysis: Freud and the Hidden Fault of the Father.* Baltimore, MD: Johns Hopkins, 1982.

Bartley, William Warren. *The Retreat to Commitment.* La Salle, IL: Open Court, 1984.

_____. *Unfathomed Knowledge, Unmeasured Wealth.* La Salle, IL: Open Court, 1990.

Bennett, William J. *The Book of Virtues.* New York: Simon & Schuster, 1994.

_____. *The De-Valuing of America.* New York: Summit, 1992.

_____. *Our Children and Our Country.* New York: Simon & Schuster, 1989.

Berry, John N. "Senator McCain's Phony 'Protection'." *Library Journal* 15 March 1998: 6.

Bettig, Ronald V. *Copyrighting Culture: The Political Economy of Intellectual Property.* Boulder, CO: Westview Press, 1996.

Bloom, Allan. *The Closing of the American Mind.* New York: Simon & Schuster, 1987.

Bloom, Howard. *The Lucifer Principle: A Scientific Expedition into the Forces of History.* New York: Atlantic Monthly, 1997.

Booth, Pat. *All for Love.* New York: Crown, 1993.

Broadfield, A. *A Philosophy of Librarianship.* London: Grafton, 1949.

Bufe, Charles. *Alcoholics Anonymous: Cult or Cure?* Tucson, AZ: See Sharp Press, 1991.

Burnham, James. *Suicide of the West.* Washington, DC: Regnery, 1985.

Caputi, Jane. *The Age of Sex Crime.* Bowling Green, OH: Popular Press, 1987.

Cosgrove, Michael H. *The Cost of Winning: Global Development Policies and Broken Social Contracts.* New Brunswick (U.S.A.): Transaction Pub., 1996.

Davis, Kenneth C. *Don't Know Much About the Civil War.* Fairfield, NJ: Morrow, 1996.

Davis, Kenneth S. *Kansas: A Bicentennial History.* New York: Norton, 1976.

Delany, Samuel R. *Mad Man.* New York: Masquerade, 1996.

Eco, Umberto. *The Name of the Rose.* New York: Harcourt Brace, 1994.

Ehrman, Bart D. *The Orthodox Corruption of Scripture.* New York: Oxford Univ. Press, 1993.

Ellis, Bret Easton. *American Psycho: A Novel.* New York: Random, 1991.

_____. *The Informers.* New York: Knopf, 1994.

Faulkner, Claude W. *Writing Good Sentences.* New York: Macmillan, 1973.

Fillion, Kate. *Lip Service.* New York: HarperCollins, 1996.

Gingrich, Newt. *Contract with America.* Westminster, MD: Times Books, 1994.

Graham, Lloyd. *Deceptions and Myths of the Bible.* Secaucus, NJ: Citadel, 1989.

Gray, John. *Mars and Venus in the Bedroom.* New York: HarperCollins, 1995.

Hellinger, Daniel, and Dennis R. Judd. *The Democratic Facade.* Belmont, CA: Wadsworth, 1994.

Home, Stewart. *No Pity.* San Francisco: AK Press, 1993.

Howells, William Dean. *The Rise of Silas Lapham.* New York: Oxford Univ. Press, 1997.

Irokawa, Daikichi. *The Age of Hirohito*. New York: Free Press, 1995.

Jackson, John. *The Black Book of Revenge*. New York: Barricade, 1992.

Jeansonne, Glen. *Gerald L.K. Smith: Minister of Hate*. New Haven: Yale, 1988.

Joyce, Davis D., ed. *An Oklahoma I Had Never Seen Before: Alternative Views of Oklahoma History*. Norman: Univ. of Oklahoma Press, 1994.

Kersten, Holger, and Elmar R. Gruber. *The Jesus Conspiracy: The Turin Shroud and the Truth About Resurrection*. Shaftsbury, Dorset; Rockport, MA: Element, 1994.

Kinsella, Kevin G., and Yvonne J. Gist. *Older Workers, Retirement, and Pensions: A Comparative International Chartbook*. Washington, DC: U.S. Dept. of Commerce, Economics and Statistics Administration, Bureau of the Census, 1995.

Korten, David C. *When Corporations Rule the World*. West Hartford, CT: Kumarian Press; Berrett-Koehler, 1995.

Kurtz, Paul. *The Transcendental Temptation: A Critique of Religion and the Paranormal*. Buffalo, NY: Prometheus Books, 1986.

Lacarriere, Jacques. *The Gnostics*. San Francisco: City Lights, 1989.

Leuthold, David A. *Campaign Missouri 1992*. Columbia: Univ. of Missouri Press, 1994.

Lind, Michael. *The Next American Nation*. New York: Free Press, 1995.

Loewen, James W. *Lies My Teacher Told Me*. New York: New Press, 1995.

MacDonald, Andrew. *The Turner Diaries: A Novel*. New York: Barricade Books, 1996.

Masson, Jeffrey Moussaieff. *Assault on Truth: Freud's Suppression of the Seduction Theory*. New York: Penguin, 1985, c1984.

McDowell, Josh. *Evidence That Demands a Verdict*. Nashville, TN: Nelson, 1993.

McWilliams, Wilson Carey, and Michael T. Gibbons, eds. *The Federalists, the Antifederalists, and the American Political Tradition*. New York: Greenwood, 1992.

Melville, Herman. *The Confidence Man*. Amherst, NY: Prometheus, 1995.

Mitchell, Margaret. *Gone with the Wind*. New York: Macmillan, 1936.

Parenti, Michael. *Inventing Reality: The Politics of News Media*. New York: St. Martin's Press, 1993.

Priestley, Joseph. *Political Writings*. Cambridge: Cambridge Univ. Press, 1993.

Rand, Ayn. *The Fountainhead*. New York: Signet, 1996.

Reed, John. *Ten Days That Shook the World*. New York: Modern Library, 1960.

Rivers, Caryl. *Slick Spins and Fractured Facts: How Cultural Myths Distort the News*. New York: Columbia Univ. Press, 1996.

Salibi, Kamal. *Conspiracy in Jerusalem*. London: Tauris, 1990.

Santoro, Victor. *Gaslighting: How to Drive Your Enemies Crazy*. Port Townsend, WA: Loompanics, 1994.

Shenkman, Richard, and George McKeon. *Legends, Lies & Cherished Myths of World History*. New York: HarperPerennial, 1994.

Silverstein, Charles. *The New Joy of Gay Sex*. New York: HarperPerennial, 1993

Sinclair, Upton. *Upton Sinclair's The Jungle: The Lost First Edition*. Ed. Gene DeGruson. Memphis: Peachtree/St. Lukes, 1988 (also called *The Lost First Edition of Upton Sinclair's The Jungle*).

Smith, Hendrick. *Rethinking America*. New York: Random House, 1995.

Smith, Morton. *Clement of Alexandria and the Secret Gospel of Mark*. Cambridge: Harvard Univ. Press, 1973.

_____. *Jesus the Magician*. San Francisco: Harper & Row, 1981.

Szabo, Ervin. *Socialism and Social Science*. London: Routledge & Kegan Paul, 1982.

Trenchard, John, and Thomas Gordon. *Cato's Letters*. Indianapolis, IN: Liberty Fund, 1995.

_____, and _____. *The English Libertarian Heritage*. San Francisco, CA: Fox & Wilkes, 1994.

Walmsley, Tom. *Shades*. Vancouver, BC: Arsenal, 1993.

Waugh, Thomas. *Hard to Imagine*. New York: Columbia Univ. Press, 1996.

Weaver, Paul H. *News and the Culture of Lying*. New York: Free Press, 1994.

Whistler, James A. McNeil Whistler. *Ten o'Clock; a Lecture* Girard, KS: Haldeman-Julius, 1926 (also included in *The Gentle Art of Making Enemies*).

Wills, Gary. *Inventing America*. Garden City, NY: Doubleday, 1978.

Wilson, Robert Anton, and Robert Shea. *The Illuminatus Trilogy*. New York: Dell, 1989.

Wind, Edgar. *Pagan Mysteries in the Renaissance*. New York: Norton, 1969.

Wolferen, Karel van. *The Enigma of Japanese Power: People and Politics in a Stateless Nation*. New York: Vintage, 1990.

Chapter 3

Censorship and Community Standards

"Our age might be called the apotheosis of mediocrity."
— Dean Acheson

The historic role of libraries as impartial purveyors of information has, in recent years, come under increased scrutiny, especially from various right-wing organizations, including Dr. James Dobson's Focus on the Family and its creature, Family Friendly Libraries. In recent years it has become all too clear that the supposed "impartiality" of libraries was really never more than a political fiction designed to encourage bipartisan support for libraries during the growth periods of the 1940s, 1950s, and especially the 1960s.

But during the 1970s and 80s, the bipartisan nature of library support came under increased pressure as local, state, and federal governments were motivated to reduce taxes by cutting back on expenses, and especially by cutting back on social services — including library services.

Librarians have, in fact, always been associated with the "progressive" and "liberal humanist" political values of tolerance and rationality, and especially the movement toward a more open, just, and free society. But often we have not clearly defended these values, shying away from political confrontation in the name of our cherished "impartiality." But our enemies, the forces of intolerance and irrationality, have never really been fooled by our attempts to "play possum" in the face of these political battles.

Under increased pressure to justify our existence, simply reasserting the old liberal, progressive values may not be enough. Although there has been, because of the very nature of libraries, a strong tendency to support "social responsibility," it is increasingly important that we recognize the need for political action. Librarians and library organizations have struggled for nearly a century over the need for social responsibility. The need for at least the perception of impartiality is in conflict with the desire for political action on the part of a large number of librarians.

Generally speaking, librarians support the concept of social responsibility as a sort of liberal humanist enterprise that falls within our ken as both "social" and "responsible." This means that we reserve the right to speak out as individuals and citizens on those issues that affect our communities. But we still seem to shy away from involvement with other progressive organizations, except of course when we need them to help with a local bond issue.

The most recent ballyhoo from the political Right is the call for "community standards" in deciding what should or should not go into a library's collection. This idea, like the concept of "original intent" when applied to constitutional law, is guaranteed to create a library that appeals to the lowest common denominator in the community. This appeal to community standards usually means that libraries should buy only those books that no one in the community could possibly object to.

The problem is, of course, what happens when you try to force particular titles into this category. And at this point it might be helpful to look to the past at some famous cases of censorship and near censorship, both direct and indirect, with a view toward understanding what is "objectionable" and what isn't.

LITERARY SIDELIGHTS

1748. Eighteenth century readers of Richardson's novel *Clarissa* were shocked and horrified by the rape scene. Modern readers, however, often read right past the description of Clarissa's rape without realizing what is happening.

1782. Choderlos de Laclos' novel *Les Liaisons Dangereuses* provided a perhaps all-too-realistic description of the sexual escapades of the French aristocracy. One critic found the moral views of the book's characters so reprehensible that he suggested the book be labeled "Not for internal use." Recently, however, the book has become a Broadway play and adapted as two films: *Dangerous Liaisons* and *Valmont*.

1817. Revolutionary War general "Light-Horse Harry" Lee argued with his sons that Pope's translation of *The Iliad* was the greatest poetic work in English. But his sons, including young Robert E. Lee, insisted that Milton's *Paradise Lost* was a greater poem. This change in aesthetic views at the beginning of the 19th century suggests that in some ways perhaps life does imitate art. Earlier, in the 17th century John Milton had participated in the revolution that overthrew Charles I of England. After the revolution collapsed with the restoration of Charles II to the throne, Milton went into political exile and wrote *Paradise Lost*. His reputation languished for over a century before he was rehabilitated in the Romantic Era by readers like the young Robert E. Lee. Years later, when the younger General Lee was offered command of the Union army, he declined, perhaps unconsciously following Milton's lead in this decision. Oddly enough, the American Civil War was later referred to by one historian as "An American Iliad."

1855. Walt Whitman sent a copy of his poems *Leaves of Grass* to poet and critic James Russell Lowell, who was so offended by the frank descriptions of the human body that he took the book and flung it into the fireplace. Even though Whitman offended many American readers, in England a group of admirers formed, including the Irish novelist Bram Stoker. A Canadian doctor, Richard M. Bucke, read *Leaves of Grass* and experienced a Pentecostal religious epiphany. He then wrote a book *Cosmic Consciousness* that claimed Whitman was an enlightened spiritual teacher, in the tradition of Moses, Christ, and Dante.

1857. Herman Melville's last novel *The Confidence Man, His Masquerade* was published. Like *Moby Dick* and *Pierre*, this book was a commercial failure, and Melville abandoned his literary career, becoming a civil servant. Melville's 19th century audience enjoyed his early seafaring novels, but not his later satiric work. His reputation has now come full circle, and today he is widely considered America's greatest novelist.

19th century. Latin was a common subject in schools through the end of the century. Because many of the great Latin authors wrote obscene and scandalous satires against their enemies, many publishers decided that it was necessary to cut these passages and move them to an appendix section at the end of school Latin textbooks. Of course, this practice made it just that much easier for English schoolboys to find and read "the naughty bits."

19th century. Writers from the Restoration and 18th century were especially popular with Victorian schoolboys because of their graphic and humorous treatment of human sexual activities. Oddly enough, Swift's *Gulliver's Travels* was a favorite with schoolboys, and many slang expressions were drawn from it, including a few obscene ones. Today, most people think of this satire as a delightful children's story, and there are numerous cartoon versions and, more recently, a made-for-TV version starring Ted Danson (but without the scatology).

1907. British novelist Elinor Glyn's scandalous novel *Three Weeks* included a description of a romantic tryst on a tiger-skin rug. The book so shocked the catalogers at the Library of Congress that they didn't create a title card for the book in the library's card catalog, presuming that only patrons who could remember the author's name needed access to the book. Despite the fact that Elinor Glyn is the literary ancestor of Jacqueline Susann, modern readers would find this book much less titillating than the average modern romance novel.

1953. Ernest Hemingway was awarded the Pulitzer Prize for fiction. The award was denied Hemingway for many years because of the sexual nature of his short story "Up in Michigan." The Pulitzer was forthcoming only because it was clear that Hemingway was about to receive the Nobel Prize, and it was felt that he had to receive the Pulitzer Prize first or the Pulitzer committee would be embarrassed internationally for not recognizing Hemingway's work.

The point of each of these examples it that literary tastes can change wildly from place to place and era to era, and the fate of an author's reputation or a particular work may lie more with chance or politics, rather than any intrinsic merit. What is more important is that some works managed to persist, finding an audience in spite of neglect or the efforts of censors. The question I would like to explore is this: Why do certain works persist in spite of opposition from censors or adverse criticism? The answer to the question goes to the heart of how we view ourselves as a society, moving toward the end of the millennium.

Earlier, during the first half of this century, social critics generally assumed that the United States was not really an aristocracy (at least not in the British model) where important decisions were made by the powerful elite. This was in spite of the growing power of men like Rockefeller and Carnegie. It was only later, with the publication of Bruno Rizzi's *The Bureaucratization of the World* (1939), that social scientists began to recognize the growing influence of a bureaucratic elite in both government and corporations. Rather crudely, social critics of the postwar era jumped to the conclusion that we live in a society based on merit, and that the United States was a "meritocracy" (as it was called by the pundits at Harvard and elsewhere who were struggling to justify their continued existence, in spite of the leveling social forces unleashed at the end of World War II).

In contrast to this fabled Meritocracy, I would like to suggest that we actually live in a "Mediocracy"—that is, a society controlled by mediocrities. Something like this was hinted at in the play *Amadeus*, where the composer Salieri proclaims himself to the audience as the "Patron Saint of Mediocrities." In the play it is Salieri who controls Mozart's life and fortunes. It is Salieri, and his ilk, who control the direction of art by controlling access to money, patronage, and social acceptance. This means that the decisions about what is good music, what is good art, what is good literature — these decisions are not controlled by artists, or at least not by good artists. Rather the decisions about who will get grants, who will get published, who will get exhibitions, who will get reviews — all these decisions, which have enormous ramifications for the future of art — all these decisions are made by mediocrities (Marquis, page 68).

Anyone today who works in a large corporation or in government can see these forces at work on a daily basis. We live in the empire of the managerial elite, though the word "elite" should not be taken to mean that these people have any special skills or abilities. Rather, these bureaucratic managers have their origins in the way small bands of hunters in the primeval forests were organized, where the delicate art of bum-sniffing had its first flowering and where learning how to trick someone else into running under the belly of the great woolly mammoth often meant the difference between life and death. With the coming of civilization, these same skills were finely honed and developed, so that again the leaders of the herd were those who were best at getting someone else to attack the gates of the city, or charge point-blank into the cannons at Waterloo. The mediocrities of the world came into their own with the development of civilization, and they have pretty much been running things to suit themselves ever since.

The consequences of this for literature, art and other forms of artistic expression have been dismal. In the past, a Beethoven or Mozart could go off into his corner and compose, perhaps even make a modest living by occasionally pandering to the powerful elites. At one time or another during their careers, all the famous artists have had to learn how to get along with the Mediocracy. The exceptions are people like Blake or Melville, who mainly had to wait for posthumous recognition. In fact, most artists have to wait until they are dead to receive recognition — the credit then goes to the mediocrity who was clever enough to dig them up and promote their work.

In terms of popular culture, the Mediocracy tends to favor its own. Popular writers seem invariably to be those writers who are able to attract a mass audience, but with a prose style that rarely moves beyond a sixth grade level and plots and characters that appeal to the prejudices of the audience. For example, one of America's best-selling authors (over 2.5 million copies sold) is Pat Booth, whose novels, like *Miami*, appeal to an audience of middle-aged women by using romantic (i.e., "steamy") love stories and exotic settings.

I sat down with Booth's novel *All for Love* and tried to discover what it was about the book that might appeal to her readers. The characters were essentially cardboard figures drawn from the author's life experiences as a model and photographer. The plot revolved around a medical student, Tari Jones, who meets a handsome actor on a plane and becomes romantically involved with him. Then she discovers that she has the power to heal people (or direct God to heal people) through prayer. At the same time she is engaged in a heated, passionate sexual relationship with the actor. Toward the end of the book Tari, an orphan, comes to discover that her long-lost father is actually a billionaire, and she quickly comes into an enormous fortune. Finally, a group of evil psychiatrists, who had planned to institutionalize Tari, are forced to abandon this plan after the Justice Department threatens legal action against them for violating Tari's civil rights. Obviously, any one of these events would stretch the credulity of a moderately intelligent person to the breaking point, but this criticism is valid only if we assume that Booth's readers are approaching this book as rational agents. Even if we assume that readers expect a certain amount of fantasy in their romance, this book goes way overboard.

The reviewer for *Booklist* (which, as we all know, is very selective, and a published review constitutes an endorsement of the book for purchase by libraries) describes *All for Love* as "gripping and neatly crafted" and "a fascinating story." I would submit that the words "fantastic" or "ridiculous" should be substituted for "fascinating." This book is fascinating only in the way a train wreck is fascinating. The reviewer for *Publishers Weekly* was a little less kind, saying that *All for Love* "nicely captures the glitzy aura of Miami's trendy South beach" but the plot reaches "new heights of absurdity"—which leads me to believe that Pat Booth may have a chronic problem with her plots. However, from the standpoint of the librarian reading *Booklist* or the bookstore owner reading *Publishers Weekly* the issue is less the moronic plot than the fact that people will, in spite of the poor writing, want to read this book. The quality of the writing is irrelevant to the desires of the great mass of readers who, responding to the media blitz, will buy or check out this book.

A similar point could be made about the books written by Stephen King. In fact, King's writing style is at best pedestrian, with little to recommend it in the way of language or characterization. His plots are sometimes fairly clever, but somehow I doubt that he ever rises above the inventiveness of Ms. Booth when it comes to creating a world of pure fantasy. In terms of writing ability, Stephen King is certainly not even playing in the same ballpark as Dan Simmons, S.P. Somtow, and dozens of other less well-known authors.

Every time the publishing industry promotes a Pat Booth or a Stephen King, it produces great leveling forces in the literary world. Success breeds imitation, and there are many young writers who try to imitate what has already succeeded. Some of these forces are not only leveling, they are downright corrupting, just like using classical music to sell soft drinks.

In much the same fashion, art styles and famous art works are appropriated for advertisements. The Impressionist painting *The Scream* was brought to life through computer animation and used in television ads to sell automobiles. Similarly, a computer-generated Fred Astaire is now selling vacuum cleaners in a television ad. It has gotten to the point where advertising is feeding on popular culture to the point we don't know where one stops and the other starts. Our culture has been reduced to an advertisement.

I own an old Pepsi can that uses pop art–style neon letters. Of course, some people would argue that pop art has strong historical ties to advertising, and therefore I shouldn't complain. But the interesting thing about my Pepsi can is that its design spells "sex" in neon colored letters. You can only read the word "sex" if you turn the can 360 degrees, but when you look at a display of cans stacked up, the "sex" is a lot easier to see. I assume that Pepsi intended this to be a subliminal message, like the "sox" on the popular baseball cap; but so many people saw the "sex" in a nonsubliminal way that the Pepsi distributor pulled the cans and canceled the design. The question is, then, should we complain about using pop art to sell soft drinks, or should we complain about using subliminal sexual messages to sell soft drinks?

The recent vogue of books on cassette is another corrupting influence, because of the focus on mass marketing — that is, popular literature is often good literature that has been "popularized" or dumbed down to reach a larger audience. But of all these influences, the one I dislike the most is the recent trend of creating novelizations of movies that were already based on classic novels, yet this has happened already with *The Scarlet Letter*, *Little Women*, and *Dracula*. The reason for this is purely commercial. Since the movie company can't copyright *The Scarlet Letter*, they have to create a new version as the movie tie-in. Also, since the movie's plot usually bears little resemblance to the original novel, it may be necessary for the movie company to create a novelization just to protect themselves from criticism. At the same time, I don't appreciate their calling a book *Bram Stoker's Dracula* when, in fact, it bears little resemblance to Bram Stoker's *Dracula*.

I don't mean to single out Stephen King or Pat Booth for ridicule, as their writing is well within the current standards for popular fiction. As popular as their books are, it would be hard to argue that these books do not constitute a "community standard" of sorts that covers most of the United States of Mediocracy. Still, Booth's *All for Love* describes scenes of wild sexual abandon, including a scene where Tari, overwhelmed by her feelings, begins masturbating in a hallway. This book goes far beyond many "classic" books that are still frequently challenged as "obscene." But issues of obscenity and censorship are rarely raised with contemporary popular fiction, except fiction geared toward children and young adults. It strikes me as odd that a book like *Catcher in the Rye* is still being challenged in libraries, while books like Pat Booth's *All for Love* are generally ignored, as if there are no young adults who might read this book. And why is this?

Each year bookstores in this country go through a ritual, coordinated by the American Library Association, called the "celebration" of Banned Books Week. Typically, the bookstore in your local mall sets up a "Banned Books" display near the front entrance of the store. The store hasn't actually bought any new "controversial" books, like Thomas Disch's *The Priest*, or *Empire of the Senseless*, or *The Wild Boys*, or *Querelle*, or *The Secret Gospel of Judas of Kerioth*. Instead they pulled a few "classic" titles, like *Catcher in the Rye* or *The Grapes of Wrath*, that have been "challenged" in some library in some hick town somewhere and move them to a display at the front of the store.

In what possible way can *Catcher in the Rye* be considered a banned book? It's easily available in several different editions and in many different languages. It's frequently taught in public schools. Virtually every bookstore in America has copies on the shelf. *Catcher in the Rye* is no more "banned" than *The Bible* or *The Koran*. Yet, like Rushdie's books, they were banned somewhere else, so we can show how enlightened and superior we are to the clerics in Iran or the Yahoos in some genetic backwater in the Mississippi Delta. Once banned books week is over, the bookstore in the mall will move the titles from the display back to the shelves and life will go on.

This is little more than an exercise in self-congratulation, an ego trip for the success of "liberalism" and "diversity." Wow! We actually moved *A Raisin in the Sun* from the shelves in the back of the store to a display out front — an open invitation to the KKK to burn a cross in front of our store in the mall. What courage! Viva Democracy! Viva Liberty!

Someone like myself might question the need for such mock celebrations, but evidently many bookstores and libraries take these things quite seriously. On the one hand, a display of "banned" classics throws into sharp relief the absurdity of most efforts to censor literature, but on the other hand our "celebration" is more exclusive than inclusive when it comes to celebrating so-called "radical" or "controversial" books. For example, I don't think I've ever seen any S&M erotica on a banned books display (not counting William S. Burroughs' well-known "classic" *Naked Lunch*). Similarly, only bookstores and libraries that cater to the homosexual community are likely to include the annual *Best Gay Erotica* or *Best Lesbian Erotica* on their displays, even when they have books like *The Joy of Sex* or *Best American Erotica* on their shelves year round.

Books describing homosexual relationships, or forms of what might be called "aberrant" sexual behavior, even when dealt with in a very circumspect way (as for example *Lolita*), are obvious targets for censorship, while "steamy" and "explicit" books showing conventional sexual relationships (even when using graphic descriptions of what most censors would call "fornication" or "adulterous relationships") are generally accepted and virtually ignored by the censors. Even in the rare occasions when a book like *American Psycho* comes under fire, the publisher will come to its defense like a bulldog defending a bone. The only explanation for this is that the Mediocracy protects its own. Furthermore, many thousands of dollars ride on the success of the latest trashy novel written by Pat Booth, and so the Mediocracy has a major financial interest in her success.

I also wonder about how a book like *Huckleberry Finn* becomes a target for censors. There may be occasional challenges when a public school considers using *Huck Finn* as a text in literature classes. Often, African American parents start a protest, claiming that this book uses the "n" word and portrays blacks in an unflattering light. I, as well as many other people, may see some merit in this claim. However, the use of the word *nigger* can be defended on historical grounds, as this term was in common usage at the time the book was written. At the same time, a mature reader can see that, on the whole, the character of Jim is portrayed in this book as a much more sympathetic character than either Huck or Tom Sawyer. Frankly, Jim is portrayed in a more sympathetic light than most of the characters in any of Twain's other books, too. Critics tend to forget that, after all, Mark Twain was a satirist and humorist.

To some extent I think that some African American parents object to *Huck Finn* as part of their own little mock exercise. On the one hand, they know that the school is unlikely to drop *Huck Finn*, since it is a classic novel and dropping the book would leave the school open to ridicule from other schools and criticism from the ACLU and other liberal organizations. At the same time, protesting the use of *Huck Finn* helps to serve notice to schoolteachers and administrators that black families are keeping tabs on them and on the textbooks they use. So, in fact, the effort to "ban" *Huck Finn* is really a ritualized combat in which both sides already know the outcome. No one seriously believes that *Huck Finn* is in any danger of being removed from school libraries (although the school may later quietly drop it from the curriculum). As a classic American novel this book is a "safe" target for parents who want to let the school administration know they are there, much like a shot fired across the bow. In fact, the real target is probably some other issue with racial overtones that has recently come up; *Huck Finn* is just a convenient target.

A more interesting case is the novel *Our Nig* (1859), generally considered the first novel written by an African American woman. This book was unpopular when it was written, largely because it criticized the way Northern whites treated their black servants. Coming as it did, at the beginning of the Civil War, it was sure to be less popular than *Uncle Tom's Cabin*, a more luridly sentimental novel which focused on the inhumane way Southern whites treated their slaves. The novel *Our Nig* soon fell into obscurity, where it stayed, even after the efforts in the early part of this century to rediscover early black novels. The reason for this, it has been suggested, is that the book includes an interracial marriage. Because racial intermarriage is still a serious social issue that causes a good deal of discomfort, with both races, this book may have been neglected intentionally. And so, only recently has *Our Nig* finally been rediscovered and reprinted.

Essentially, any literary novel that has achieved some status as a "classic" is held to a very different standard than the standards used for contemporary popular fiction. People are more likely to object to the sexual descriptions in *Gravity's Rainbow* than they are to the passionate sexual descriptions that appear in hundreds of contemporary novels written in the Romance genre.

The reason for this is clear. What can be "shown" in a novel is a fashion that changes over time. While Elinor Glyn's 1907 novel *Three Weeks* might have been considered obscene in its day, today it would probably not even make a contemporary reader blush. The reasons for censorship have little to do with how much flesh is exposed or how explicit the sex may be. Rather, censorship has to do with how a book challenges the status quo. While "a glimpse of stocking" might threaten the powers-that-be in the Victorian Era, contemporary power relationships are not easily threatened by even the most explicit sexual acts. Sexual acts that involve group sex, homosexuality, or "aberrant" forms of sexuality are still considered a minor threat, but I suspect that this is because people who are "aberrant" in their sexuality are also very often aberrant in their lifestyles and their politics.

Both sides of the Culture War use classic literature for their own ends. A conservative publisher might bring out new editions of standard conservative works, like Ayn Rand's *We the Living*. Similarly, a liberal publisher recently brought out a collection of Whitman's poetry that included homoerotic drawings. And so, during periods of political upheaval, aberrant old "classics" like *The Leaves of Grass*, *The Fountainhead*, and *Walden* achieve a renewed audience and a renewed interest, right along with *On the Road* and *Howl*. They often become the center of more mock political battles, as partisans on the Left and Right fire potshots at each other.

The status quo no longer perceives *Lady Chatterley's Lover*, *Les Liaisons Dangereuses*, or *Three Weeks* as a serious threat to existing power relationships. Other books, like *The Grapes of Wrath* or *Catcher in the Rye*, are still considered threats because of their political message. Famous political novels, like Turgenev's *Fathers and Sons* or Stendhal's *The Red and the Black*, continue to be dangerous, even after the particular political events that brought them into being have long passed.

Political change is inevitable, and the arts tend to exist on the cutting edge of political change. The relationship between political change and artistic change may have been more obvious in the era of Percy Bysshe Shelley, Mary Shelley and William Godwin, but there is still a clear connection. Past generations may look to Pope's *Iliad* for its ideals, or it may look further back to Milton's *Paradise Lost*, but it is a certainty that creative thinkers will always look to the past for models. They look for the inspiration that will lead them on to new artistic conquests.

After all, if a minor classic like *The Jungle* can cause a public outcry that forces the passage of federal pure food laws, and if a mediocre novel like *The Turner Diaries* can lead to death and destruction in a federal building in Oklahoma City, then what might happen when the next generation's version of *Catcher in the Rye* is written? Perhaps the clerics in Iran were right about *The Satanic Verses* after all, as Rushdie's works, at least to the extent they may challenge Islamic fundamentalism, may be a real threat to their regime. Like Tom Paine, Salman Rushdie's real crime was inciting revolution, not blasphemy.

Political stability, which usually means political stagnation, serves the interests of the Mediocracy. And so the Mediocracy will struggle with all its power to control and channel the arts in ways that tend to diminish the political effect of their artistic message. This is why there is so much controversy over NEA funding of the arts. On the one hand, liberals perceive the need for federal funding and its moderating influence on artistic expression. On the other hand, conservatives don't like the arts at all, and especially the "liberal" arts. Conservatives like the idea of impoverished wild-eyed artists who advocate revolution, the better to justify crushing them. Similarly, they like having controversial artists around, because it gives them the chance to score political points against liberals. And so the war of the books is still very much with us.

That great works of literature ever achieve recognition is a monument not to the civilization of Mediocracy but to the stubborn power of art to find its way, no matter what. And for every Blake or Melville or Stoddard who finds her way out of obscurity, there are thousands more who are buried forever in the muck. The world of publishing is not geared to support excellence in literature, and literary recognition tends to happen by accident if at all.

Many people seem to think that creative artists can find a home in higher education where they can practice their art and find a comfortable niche from which both to teach and to write or paint or compose or engage in a creative enterprise. And to some limited extent this is true, as a few universities have come to act as patrons for a few writers and artists (though usually those artists who are already famous and well beyond their prime get the plum jobs). Universities can serve to support the arts, though usually in a minor way. Again, their role is limited, since the universities are also bastions of mediocrity and primarily exist to serve the needs of this same Mediocracy (Bartley, pages 95–149).

Some people think that a creative person can be published and receive a measure of success solely through the system of higher education. This is wrong. Except for a few "prestige" schools, interest in the arts is not encouraged to any great extent. In fact, Wallace Stevens, who wrote poetry while working for an insurance company, probably had more encouragement than most creative artists receive through a career in higher education. For example, I know of one English teacher in a college in the Midwest who writes poetry and has been fairly successful in getting it published. Her department chair also writes poetry, but he has been singularly unsuccessful in getting anything published. And so he, of course, is the only one who gets to teach the creative writing classes. And every time she has a book published or gets a big-name writer to visit campus, he responds by trying to get the vice president to fire her. This may be an extreme case, but professional envy does play a big role when it comes time to discuss promotion and tenure on most college campuses. This not only applies to creative endeavors, but also to scholarship and research endeavors, too. Writers who have any ability at all would do well to lie low until after they have tenure.

The power of the Mediocracy usually goes unrecognized, especially when it extends into higher education. For example, critics of higher education usually focus on the Harvards, the Yales, the Stanfords, and ignore what goes on in the smaller, less prestigious colleges and universities. Although it may be true that at Yale research and scholarship can lead to special perks and privileges, including a raise or a reduced class load, that is not the case at most colleges. This is an important distinction. With scholarship, as with art, the rewards and money are still controlled by the Mediocracy, and the Mediocracy is loath to let any of it pass outside its little circle of friends.

The Mediocracy at the major universities controls the boards of prestigious journals, the editorial boards of major publishers and scholarly presses, and the publications of most learned societies. Publishing opportunities are doled out as rewards to the friends of the editorial board, and rarely does anything make its way into print without their dubious stamp of approval. It's been years since I've seen an article in a literary journal that was readable, let alone interesting in its subject matter. And this is in a discipline which is supposed to have some connection to the teaching of writing! The writing style and verbiage is geared to an insider group and designed to exclude the uninitiated. After all, can you imagine Dr. Samuel Johnson trying to read the table of contents page of any "learned" publication put out in the discipline of English today?

At the typical state university, other than the flagship institutions, the rewards for scholarship are little or none. In fact, at most institutions scholarship can be said to be tolerated rather than encouraged — a hobby or personal peculiarity of the eccentric professor. I think it's fair to say that a professor is rarely dismissed from one of these institutions for having scholarly standards that are too low (Bartley, page 118). And a new faculty member at one of these institutions would be well advised to forget scholarship, except for presentations at conventions and a few papers in minor publications, at least until he or she has tenure. The fact is that the smaller universities encourage scholarship only to the extent that it is necessary for certifying certain specific programs and for maintaining their accreditation.

The same Mediocracy controls the administration of these universities, and these administrators are unlikely to recognize, let alone reward, any activity that they do not themselves engage in. For example, at most of these smaller universities the activity of presenting a paper at a regional convention is considered to be of equal importance to publishing a paper in a reputable scholarly journal. There are, of course, no standards to be met in presenting a paper at most of these regional conventions, except the willingness to show up and read for ten minutes. Over the years I've seen honors and rewards passed out to faculty for taking classes on field trips, or serving as an officer in a regional organization, or making a presentation at a regional convention, while other faculty were ignored who were doing serious scholarship on a national level. The reason for this is clear.

Although most administrators may be able to teach a class or two with a minimal amount of effort, the ability to write a coherent paper and get it accepted in a scholarly journal is beyond the best efforts of the typical administrator. Unless you have an impressive skill, it is hard to get published, especially when most learned journals are controlled by the big universities and serve the interests of their faculty.

Since none of these administrators get published in reputable journals, publication obviously can have no value to the university. It may seem hard to believe, but in most small universities a speech presented at the local Kiwanis meeting carries as much weight, in terms of getting promotion and tenure, as a presentation before a meeting of a national learned society. Standards to measure the quality of research do not exist, and there is considerable political pressure on campus to keep it that way. The university may give a good deal of lip service to the need for research and scholarship, but it won't put much in the way of financial incentives behind such talk. The smaller colleges and universities promote scholarship only to the extent that they are forced to do so by accrediting agencies and governing boards.

Just as the common assumptions about scholarship in universities are mostly wrong, so is the assumption that universities are bastions of left liberalism. There are plenty of right-wing pundits who like to portray universities as bastions of "socialism" or even "communist ideals." This notion is laughable. Although it may have had some element of truth in the early part of this century, today it is wholly false, and I doubt that it has had any truth since the 1950s.

While it is true that the faculty and perhaps even a majority of students in the typical university are a bit more liberal than the people in the local community, this doesn't really mean very much. The average faculty member in a school in the South, the Midwest, or the Southwest is probably more conservative than the average factory worker, day laborer or shopkeeper in Boston. In fact, during the 1930s it was fairly typical for faculty in the South and Midwest to also be members of the Ku Klux Klan. Today, the average faculty member in the South and Southwest is certainly more conservative politically than the average union worker who works on the docks on either coast.

Recently, while attending a convention in another state, I met a graduate student who was in the process of applying for a position at a small junior college campus near where I work. She asked me about the politics of the department where she was applying. I replied that "politically, they are slightly to the right of Attila the Hun" and suggested that she spin her application accordingly. I believe that she followed my advice, showing up for her interview in a conservative dress. A few days later they offered her the job (and this was out of a pool of nearly fifty applicants).

The lesson here is that graduate students who assume all universities are "liberal" and emphasize their own liberalism will be at a serious disadvantage in the job market. I've heard of search committees who count it against a candidate if she has taken courses that sound "feminist" or if she studied "theory" too much, and this attitude is common, especially in the sciences. But the liberal arts programs are filled with reactionaries, too. Some departments in liberal arts are particularly prone to hiring the loudest, most obnoxious candidate who applies. I suspect that if a few more department chairmen were more secure in their masculinity they would not be so quick to hire the first candidate who comes into the room beating his chest and making ape-like grunts and shrieks. Personally, based on some of the candidates I've seen in recent years, I think most schools could save money by running an ad that reads:

> Wanted: Loud-mouth ignoramus of the Rush Limbaugh persuasion. Ph.D. required, conservatives preferred, knowledge and teaching ability optional (but may count against). Only self-styled intellectuals need apply.

This ad covers all the essentials and it is honest, which is why it would never be run. Ads for administrative positions could include the line: KNEE-JERK REACTIONARIES ARE ENCOURAGED TO APPLY.

No one realizes that the Mediocracy has enjoyed its own form of affirmative action for centuries. This is part of why it hates government-imposed affirmative action programs so much. These programs interfere with the Mediocracy's own much more aggressive good-old-boy hiring practices.

Another serious mistake that job candidates make is to assume that a department is interested in increasing its standards or making intellectual demands of its students. In fact, most colleges and universities have been under constant pressure for 30 years to *lower* standards and eliminate "quality" from the curriculum. Richard Mitchell, William Bartley, Reginald Damerell, and other critics recognized and commented on this problem long before William J. Bennett jumped on the bandwagon.

Recently, at a faculty senate meeting, I was the lone voice protesting when the School of Education wanted to remove a requirement that all education majors have at least a C− average in their courses outside of education. One education professor, visibly angry that I spoke against the proposal, loudly proclaimed that such a requirement would have kept him out of teaching (and, believe me, I really had to bite my tongue to avoid saying what I thought of that argument). When I asked why the School of Education wanted the requirement removed, since any student affected by the rule could have appealed to the dean of Education for a waiver, the argument was that all the other schools in the regents system had already gotten rid of the rule (meaning: When all else fails, appeal to the wisdom of the herd). Needless to say, mine was the only vote against this proposal.

The fact that students could apply for a deferral of this requirement would seem, to most rational people, to be a sufficient way of dealing with this problem. At least this was true in the past. But today it is important to avoid hurting a student's self-esteem, and so we don't want to draw attention to his or her D+ (or less) G.P.A. by making him ask for a deferral. At least this is the latest "educational thinking" (another oxymoron) in use in schools today.

Although William Bennett and dozens of other critics have written weighty tomes complaining about the quality of education in this country, there is really a fairly simple answer to the problem. All you have to do is improve teacher education. Several critics, some writing more than 20 years ago, recognized that this is the main problem with our educational system. In fact, you can learn more from reading Gene Lyons' essay "Why Teachers Can't Teach" (pages 186–211) than you can from reading all the hysterical gloom-and-doom books written during the intervening 20 years. The real problem is that the political Right wants to privatize education in order to break the teacher's unions, while the Left can't afford to alienate the teacher's unions by advocating real reforms. And so the political dance goes on and on.

Part of the difference between prominent universities and the lower or mid-level universities is created by the differences in the compensation for faculty. In academic areas, like the humanities, where there is a great deal of competition for jobs, a small college or university can afford to hire really exceptional people. But in the area of business, for example, these schools often cannot begin to compete with the financial resources of larger schools, and the quality of the faculty they can afford to hire is much lower. Yet, at the same time, it is these faculty — who are usually much better paid than the humanities faculty and who are "important" because they are "in demand" — it is these faculty members who wield a great deal of political power on campus. These faculty are also usually much more politically conservative than the rest of the campus, believing that their big salaries are justified by their greater merit. They see themselves as living proof that virtue is rewarded. And so they tend to contribute toward the rightward drift of the university. Much of what is described as the culture war on university campuses is the result of conflict between noticeably left-leaning and right-leaning departments over salaries, perks, and other privileges.

The students, however, learn to play the game fairly early. At the university where I work, the School of Business teaches a course each semester in business ethics. This is all well and good, except that every semester one of the students in this class comes into the library, does the assignment, and then hides the reference book that the other students will need to do the assignment. The student hides the book just so that the rest of the students can't get this assignment done on time. You might think this is a bit petty, but it does work. After all, the student manages to lower the grade curve, and thus gets a higher grade (as do the students who got to the material before this student did, even though they weren't "smart" or devious enough to hide the book). Several weeks later the missing reference book will turn up, and next semester we will go through the whole process again. I'm sure these students have a bright future ahead of them as part of the all-powerful Mediocracy.

Conservatives like to complain about the growing number of federal regulations, but frankly the corporate world has only itself to blame. The vast majority of regulations aimed at businesses came into being because of immoral or unethical behavior on the part of corporations, like raiding the company pension fund. Just like the student who hides the reference book, some company has taken an unethical shortcut. And the result is that the government has to create a new regulation to stop this sort of behavior. So who is to blame? The government for creating so many regulations or the corporations who are always searching for ways to trim ethics to boost their profits? I'm willing to bet that most of the whining about regulations comes from companies who didn't get a chance to take the shortcut before the regulations came into being. What's really ironic is that, in most cases, the regulations are written to include plenty of loopholes so that many companies can still find shortcuts.

The mediocrities of the world would have us believe that the real work of civilization is not art or science or philosophy, but the elaborately developed and refined art of bootlicking, the ritualized and sanitized techniques for achieving fame and fortune in the corporate or bureaucratic enterprise. So many books are written on "how to get ahead"— not to mention the seminars, tapes, and videos — that you might think this was a branch of scientific discovery all in itself, with Dale Carnegie as its patron saint. But, in fact, this noble endeavor has its roots firmly planted in the cesspool of human civilization, and not all the noble aspirations of mankind can hope to dislodge it from its place of supremacy.

The fact is, in talking about community standards, whether it is the local community or the academic community, and whether we are talking about academic standards, standards of scholarship, or political and artistic standards, it doesn't really matter — the standards that are set up are basically whatever the "leaders" of the community want them to be. When the goal is mediocrity, then the works that rise above that standard are discarded as readily as those that fall below it. Indeed, the works that rise above the standard may be actively suppressed, especially if they present ideas that challenge the status quo. And that, boys and girls, is where real censorship comes from.

This is certainly the case with the recent efforts to censor the film *The Tin Drum*. Several months ago, a judge in Oklahoma declared the film *The Tin Drum* to be pornographic and police have confiscated copies in Oklahoma City. The question is, of course, why this film is more offensive than *Pretty Baby* or, for that matter, popular films like *Fear* or *Scream* that openly exploit teenage sexuality. How else can you explain the fact that, while television networks can broadcast soap operas, dramatic series and even sitcoms that bounce sexual relationships back and forth like a ping-pong ball, a film with serious ideas and artistic merit is actively suppressed in America's heartland.

REFERENCES

Acker, Kathy. *Empire of the Senseless*. New York: Grove, 1989.

Bartley, William Warren. *Unfathomed Knowledge, Unmeasured Wealth: On Universities and the Wealth of Nations*. La Salle, IL: Open Court, 1990.

Booth, Pat. *All for Love*. New York: Crown, 1993.

Burroughs, William S. *The Wild Boys: A Book of the Dead*. New York: Grove, 1992.

Damerell, Reginald. *Education's Smoking Gun: How Teachers' Colleges Have Destroyed Education in America*. New York: Freundlich, 1985.

Disch, Thomas M. *The Priest: A Gothic Romance*. New York: Knopf, 1995.

Genet, Jean. *Querelle*. New York: Grove, 1987.

Lyons, Gene. *The Higher Illiteracy: Essays on Bureaucracy, Propaganda, and Self-Delusion*. Fayetteville: Univ. of Arkansas Press, 1988.

MacDonald, Andrew. *The Turner Diaries: A Novel*. New York: Barricade Books, 1996.

Marquis, Alice Goldfarb. *Art Lessons: Learning from the Rise and Fall of Public Arts Funding*. New York: Basic Books, 1995.

Mitchell, Richard. *The Graves of Academe*. New York: Fireside, 1987.

Rizzi, Bruno. *The Bureaucratization of the World*. New York: Free Press, 1985.

Rushdie, Salman. *The Satanic Verses: A Novel*. New York: Viking, 1989.

Selander, Maxwell, ed. *The Secret Gospel of Judas of Kerioth*. Corpus Christi: Abrasax Books, 1992.

Shaffer, Peter. *Peter Shaffer's Amadeus*. New York: Harper & Row, 1981.

Wilson, Harriet E. *Our Nig*. New York: Random, 1983.

Chapter 4

Library Automation
in the Age of Mediocrity

I would like to take a moment, using this forum, to establish my reputation for all time as one of the "Great Thinkers" of human civilization. You might think this a bit presumptuous of me; but I would argue that if I can answer questions about human nature that have eluded philosophers throughout human history, I should have a shot at the title. This seems only fair to me.

I have my own theory about the big questions of human nature. These are philosophical questions that many "Great Thinkers" have tried to answer, down through the ages. But most of them have gotten nowhere in coming up with answers. I, personally, think that it is because most philosophers are honorable men, and it is their basic virtue that has held them back from coming up with good answers to these questions. Let's face it: Anyone who spends much time contemplating "The Great Chain of Being" or "The Eternal Verities" is going to be at a serious disadvantage in answering questions about why human beings do what they do. To them, human nature will always remain a mystery.

From the standpoint of science, we need to come up with answers that can be verified through experiments and observation. Using this criterion, I would have to conclude that Machiavelli was probably the greatest philosopher of all time, surpassing even Freud and the Marquis de Sade in his understanding of human behavior. The question "why?" cannot simply be put off as an imponderable. I believe that these questions have answers; and, if you can put yourself into a truly devious mindset, you can find the answer to any question.

For example, not long ago Jeffrey Dahmer, one of the most bizarre killers of all time, was murdered in jail. The motive for the murder seems obscure, and to this day no one is quite sure exactly *why* he was killed. If, however, you consider the fact that there were a number of people associated with Dahmer after his arrest and trial who were legally or ethically prohibited from writing books and articles about Dahmer until *after* he was dead, then suddenly a likely motive for his murder becomes pretty clear.

The criteria of motive and opportunity can be applied to a whole group of activities, outside of the legal profession, which have never before been adequately questioned. In examining human behavior, including the behaviors of organizations, I believe that we need to look at motive and opportunity, rather than simply accepting the rationales we are given at face value. Nothing happens by accident; you can usually find the answer if you are willing to dig. Even fairly innocuous events have a motive. When Congress recently moved daylight savings ahead two weeks, it was because of pressure from people associated with charcoal companies (two extra weeks of families grilling food outside on the barbecue!). The motive may be good or bad, or just a chance to make a few bucks, but there is a motive, just like cause and effect in physics.

For example, during the recent controversy over outsourcing, I noted that *Library Journal* had a number of hard-hitting articles critical of outsourcing, while *American Libraries* seemed to run only articles that were conciliatory toward this practice. It would seem logical, at least to most librarians, to assume that *American Libraries*, as a publication of the American Library Association, would defend its members by going after outsourcing with a meat axe and a chain saw. This would be true, of course, only if ALA was really concerned about what was in the best interests of its members. This notion is, perhaps, about as naive as suggesting that General Motors makes corporate decisions based on what is in the best interests of its customers (pause here for laughter). Although the attitudes of the managing editors of *LJ* and *AL* toward outsourcing may be fairly similar, the approach of each publication was different. I suspect that *Library Journal* was anti-outsourcing because it represents the interests of book publishers, many of whom would be hurt by outsourcing, while *American Libraries* was going out of its way not to offend book jobbers whose financial goodwill is so important to the executives at ALA headquarters.

The same criteria can be applied to studying history. For example, why did China build the Great Wall? Why did Rome build Hadrian's Wall? Why did France build forts along the Maginot Line? None of these fortifications was particularly effective in keeping out invaders. Perhaps these monuments were more like public works projects, with bribes and money going from the communities to the central government, and government jobs flowing back to the community. Similarly, some historians now claim that most of the "injun trouble" on the American frontier was provoked by settlers because they wanted forts built and soldiers stationed in their community, with the additional influx of federal dollars. Another author suggests that the main reason for building the pyramids of Egypt was not religious. Rather, much like the work projects created by Roosevelt's New Deal, building the pyramids served to reinforce the power of the central government (Lewin, page 62).

More recently, a study written by the Defense Department's Strategic Command, called "Essentials of Post–Cold War Deterrence," makes the argument that we should maintain our gigantically expensive and powerful arsenal of atomic weapons so that we can intimidate countries like Iraq and Libya. The fact is that our nuclear weapons industry is struggling to find a justification for its continued existence. We have a host of conventional weapons that, in addition to being cheap and effective (like Whitfield's Ointment), don't leave behind an unsightly radioactive residue. But, like the Great Wall, there are strong economic motives for continuing to maintain an atomic arsenal, arguments that have little to do with common sense.

Perhaps the Military-Industrial Complex is much older than we ever imagined. If you look at warfare as a continuing process for justifying and supporting the military establishment, then the Battle of the Little Bighorn becomes simply, in terms of politics, a reenactment of the First Battle of Bull Run. In order to understand history, we need a better understanding of *why* things happen. Motive and opportunity should be explored in trying to determine the root causes for human behavior, rather than relying on rationalizations, propaganda and advertising campaigns — the traditional approach used both by journalists and historians.

For example, for some time now I've wondered why so many companies and institutions are rushing to get Windows for all their microcomputers. Perhaps it would be more accurate to say that the Systems people at these companies are pushing for Windows. Today it seems like people automatically *assume* that you will get Windows. It is a going "trend" in industry, a part of the herd-instinct of business managers all over the country. Most people would think that it has something to do with the quality of the product — at least this is the answer that Microsoft would want us to come up with. In thinking about this, though, I've come to a rather different conclusion.

Recently, the Systems librarian loaded Windows NT on my microcomputer. Shortly after installation, my library software began acting up: The screen would lock up, the print jobs took minutes rather than seconds to run, and with long print jobs (meaning more than one page) the system would sometimes lock up or throw me out of the program completely.

After looking at the computer for awhile, the Library Systems assistant decided "This is a Windows problem." His boss, the Systems librarian, agreed. This is not a problem with the library software. This is a problem with Windows. My suggestion that they take Windows off my computer collided with a blank wall. That was not an option. Rather I was promised that they would eventually look into fixing Windows.

Needless to say, I hadn't asked for Windows NT to be loaded on my microcomputer. It was the price I paid to get a new and faster computer. From the standpoint of the Systems people, the fact that my work was constantly being derailed and interrupted with computer glitches did not change the fact that I should be grateful for my new, faster microcomputer.

At the same time, Windows NT was being loaded on dozens of microcomputers in the public services area, and with similar results. Serious problems were developing for students who tried to print from the library system. And when the system locked up and threw people out, it took the intervention of the Systems assistant or one of his cohorts to get the micro unstuck and back on-line.

At this point most people would begin to question the reason why we needed to rush forward with loading Windows NT on all the workstations. I never got a convincing answer to this question. Like many other decisions made by the Systems people, it was not a decision open to question.

My own theory is that Systems people like to have Windows loaded on all their computers because then the various "bugs" in the system (and everything else they can't explain) get tagged as "a Windows problem." Similarly, automation vendors like to have Windows loaded on the terminals in the libraries they work with because it takes the pressure off them to solve problems. When things go wrong, they can blame Windows. Just think of all the money they will save on customer support! And so all the software companies are coming up with "XXX for Windows" and pushing people to run their software through Windows. And if the software doesn't run right? Hey, that's "a Windows problem."

Needless to say, if we go to Microsoft's service people, they are going to blame the software we are trying to run. This way everybody is happy, except, of course, the people who are trying to work with the software.

You might think that this is a rather paranoid view of the world. To this I would answer, "Yes, but they really are out to get me. Perhaps not me personally, but everyone like me who is at the mercy of their crummy software." But even more important, my problem with Windows is really a symptom of a much greater and more widespread problem in society.

Consider, for example, the fact that for many years people in the computer industry claimed that IBM provided the best customer support. Recently, several authors have come forward to suggest that the quality of IBM customer support was more mythical than real. The legendary IBM customer support was just that. You might ask yourself, then, "How does such a legend get started?" Let me suggest an answer.

IBM established itself fairly early in the game, but as competition grew from newer companies, the computing power of their mainframes became a bit "pricey" compared with many of their competitors. IBM salespeople responded to this challenge by using marketing techniques that were, shall we say, "aggressive" by most standards. If the person responsible for selecting and purchasing the computer hardware for a company made the "mistake" of not buying IBM, then the salespeople at IBM were not adverse to going to *his* boss and questioning his competence to make such an important decision (a book vendor I prefer not to name also uses this approach). Word soon got around in industry that IBM did not like to hear "no" from people and that the salespeople weren't shy about going over your head to your boss.

Some people, mainly the ones who were knowledgeable about computers and secure in their jobs, went ahead and bought the computer they wanted. But, at the same time, the people who were, for whatever reason, insecure in their jobs, or even incompetent to judge between one computer and another, for them IBM became the computer of choice. You can imagine the scene in the head office, months later, when some whiz-kid fresh out of college with his MBA asks the question: "Why did we buy a more expensive computer? Why didn't we buy X company's mainframe?"

The Person Responsible, stunned that anyone would question the purchase, stumbles around for an answer. Finally he says, "Well, IBM has really great customer support!"

And that's how legends get started.

Similarly, Ray Eberts has written a book called *The Myths of Japanese Quality* that, point by point, destroys the management legend that Japan has (or had) the corner on "quality." In fact, Japanese products are the result of the same shoddy workmanship that we enjoy in this country. The question is, then, how did the myth of Japanese quality get started? The answer is fairly simple. During a period of time when American corporations were losing market share to the Japanese big-time, the corporate leaders in this country had to come up with an excuse to explain the decline in American manufacturing. The obvious answer to this question is that Japanese industry was, after the economic disaster of World War II, in a better position to exploit its workers. But this is not a politically acceptable answer. How do you go to your stockholders and say, "The Japanese built their industrial empire the old-fashioned way, by screwing the workers and cutting prices." It has taken 20 years for American business to catch up to the Japanese in this area. However, it is worth noting that several large fortunes were built in this country during this same time period, particularly in the areas of chain discount stores and fast-food franchises because they developed new and better ways to exploit part-time workers. The Japanese do not have a monopoly on this method of empire building.

Corporate mythology has a logic all its own, and myths are created for a variety of reasons. David Gordon's book *Fat and Mean: The Corporate Squeeze of Working Americans and the Myth of Managerial "Downsizing"* makes the case that there has been no real downsizing of middle management. Rather, there are more managers today than there were five years ago. Instead of being a corporate trend, all this talk of "downsizing" was meant to scare lower-level white collar and blue collar workers and encourage them to have lower expectations, in terms of both compensation and working conditions. Personally, I can see this "upsizing" of management, both in salaries and numbers of positions, reflected in the state university where I work. Like Japanese "quality," the so-called downsizing of management has been a myth, albeit a useful myth for the managers.

I think it would be fair to say that the majority of decisions made in the corporate world, or in education or government, are made for reasons that have little to do with giving better service, providing quality education, or building a better mousetrap. Most decisions are made by people for their own selfish personal or political reasons that have little to do with "corporate vision" or "the public good." Most decisions have to do with "protecting one's turf" rather than the greater good of the company, agency, or enterprise of which they are a part. You might call this an "atomistic" view of how organizations function, but frankly it is safer, in trying to predict future trends for an organization, to assume that people will look out for themselves first. Corporate decisions are virtually always based on motive and opportunity.

Many people would disagree with me on this, especially people who teach courses in business ethics. I consider this area of study to be in the same league with studying the mating habits of unicorns. For a more realistic view, one need turn only to the business books written by Richard H. Buskirk over the last 30 years (e.g., *Frontal Attack, Divide and Conquer, the Fait Accompli, and 118 Other Tactics Managers Must Know*). Buskirk is a prolific author who has a refreshingly honest attitude toward the whole process of how corporations function. Similarly, you can turn to Anthony Jay's *Management and Machiavelli* for a clear view of how organizations function. More recently, Scott Bowman's *The Modern Corporation and American Political Thought* makes the case that international megacorporations are moving toward economic control of the world by subduing the power of individual national governments (which he seems to think is a good thing!).

If I were in the market for buying a stock, I would avoid companies that provide high quality goods for a cheap price. Rather, I would look for the bloated, lazy megacorporations who provide shoddy merchandise at a high price *but* have a strong marketing plan that plays on the vanity or self-interest of the people who do the buying. It works for tennis shoe manufacturers. If providing quality products at a fair price was important, a whole host of companies, from McDonald's to Target, would have gone out of business a long time ago. Better yet, look for a company that's willing to use bribery, by making large campaign contributions to politicians, in order to protect their turf and edge out the competition. This approach seems to work pretty well for library automation vendors.

In terms of how companies compete, the dinosaurs are winning out over the mammals. And until the meteor hits, the dinosaurs are going to continue running things pretty much the way they want to.

REFERENCES

Bowman, Scott R. *The Modern Corporation and American Political Thought: Law Power, and Ideology.* University Park: Penn State Univ. Press, 1996.

Buskirk, Richard Hobart. *Frontal Attack, Divide and Conquer, the Fait Accompli, and 118 Other Tactics Managers Must Know.* New York: Wiley, 1989.

Eberts, Ray E. *The Myths of Japanese Quality.* Upper Saddle River, NJ: Prentice Hall, 1995.

Gordon, David M. *Fat and Mean: The Corporate Squeeze of Working Americans and the Myth of Managerial "Downsizing."* New York: Free Press, c1996.

Jay, Anthony. *Management and Machiavelli.* New York: Holt, 1967.

Lewin, Leonard C. *Report from Iron Mountain on the Possibility and Desirability of Peace.* New York: Dell, 1967.

U.S. Strategic Command. *Essentials of Post–Cold War Deterrence.* [n.d., 1995?] Partially declassified.

Chapter 5

The Postmodern Library, or Freud in the Garden of Good and Evil

The library, as it exists today, is very much a product of modernism. The library's reason for being, as a cultural institution, usually involves the idea that humanity is enrolled in a nonracist, nonsexist, sort of universal Dale Carnegie–type improvement course. And most librarians seem to agree with this view, believing that libraries are an integral part of this ongoing project for human self-improvement and uplift. But the rise of postmodernism raises some serious questions. What happens to the library now that the project of modernism is slowly being abandoned? What happens as more and more of our popular culture reflects the views of the postmodern era? What is wrong with the modern library, and why should it think about becoming a postmodern library?

The library is a modernist project, and as such it participates in the use of discipline. According to Michel Foucault, the focus of liberal political theory under modernism was on the restraint of the political power of the monarch, but the postmodern focus is on power as it is exercised "at the capillaries." It is the technology of power, as it is exercised by the professions, that must concern us (page 89).

The rise of the professions, and the subsequent rise of the Mediocracy, has led to the exercise of power through a thousand smaller rules and regulations. Power has become a normative process, rather than a process of punishment. For example, every time a library fine is levied, it is an exercise of a normative function — an attempt to bring the individual patron into line with the expectations of the institution. This may seem a minor thing to most of us, but a similar power exercised by the IRS can become a nightmare for the individual caught up in an audit. Or better yet imagine the fate of the people at Waco who died for dealing in vaguely illegal gun purchases. Some people might prefer the good old days when all they did to you is put you on "the rack." What we need is a philosophy of librarianship designed to counter this tendency to maintain an excess of control over our collections, our patrons and ourselves. Or, as Todd May has suggested, what we need is "a politics of diffusion and multiplicity, a politics that confronts power in a variety of irreducible and often surprising places" (page 95).

The rise of the professions, and with it the rise of bureaucratic power, has come under question in recent years, and sometimes under outright criticism. Two examples will suffice to show why this has happened. Recently, Sergeant-Major Gene McKinney was tried for allegedly sexually harassing six women under his command and for obstruction of justice. A military court found him innocent of the sexual harassment charges, but convicted him on the obstruction of justice charge, primarily because the evidence of his guilt on this charge was so obvious that he could not be found "not guilty" without the military itself being charged with obstructing justice. This case bears a remarkable similarity to the original trial of the police officers charged with beating Rodney King. And it proves, once again, that an institution, or a profession, cannot regulate itself in a fair and just way.

Similarly, on the same day that Sergeant-Major McKinney received his reduction in rank, the Vatican released its long awaited statement "We Remember: A Reflection on the Shoah (Holocaust)." This document was immediately criticized by Jewish leaders as "too little, too late" and condemned by others as a whitewash of Pius XII and the role he played, or failed to play, in trying to stop the Holocaust. In some ways this document is reminiscent of the decision that came out of the Vatican a few years ago, maintaining that it was correct in it original condemnation of Galileo. The problem is that institutions, including libraries, have a difficult time criticizing themselves, let alone making changes in their practices.

Obviously, libraries need to, first, recognize that they are modernist institutions that have modernist goals and employ modernist techniques to achieve those goals. But, secondly, it is vitally important to recognize that a shift is taking place in the worldview of our culture and to position ourselves to become a part of this new age. To some extent we have done that by becoming sites where people can access the World Wide Web. But we also must realize that the postmodernist critique of modernist institutions will bring the library under greater and greater scrutiny.

The postmodernist critique has already found its way into librarianship, most notably through Sandy Berman's ongoing efforts to change Library of Congress subject headings. The use and abuse of language is a major concern of postmodernism, and Berman has maintained an ongoing project of cultural criticism aimed squarely at the ethnic, sexual, and political biases built into the subject classification scheme of the Library of Congress. My own interest is directed more toward the biases built into the Dewey classification system. For example, recently the Dewey scheme was changed so that books on the "right to life" are placed under 342.085, the number already being used for "civil rights" and racial equality. This change puts books on racial equality on the same shelf with the propaganda on fetal rights, effectively institutionalizing the pro-life view that has tried for twenty or more years to equate abortion with slavery. Similarly, when the Dewey schedule changed its standard subdivision for women from "...088042" to "...082" the result was that a lot of new books about women and women's issues ended up being buried in among a lot of old, unrelated books. This is because, up until about 1980 Dewey used "082" for collected works. So now a patron trying to find works about women, by going to the shelf, is going to have to wade through a lot of old books that have no connection to the subject at all.

Of particular importance to libraries is the growth of postmodernist thought within the profession of law, since the legal profession most clearly resembles the profession of librarianship, both in our obsession with formal rules and procedures, and the use of a standardized language. Both law and librarianship are based on formalized rules created and approved by authorities. Libraries are as dependent on AACR2 and past cataloging practices as the legal profession is dependent on Supreme Court decisions and common law. For that reason, it is worth looking at postmodernist legal theory to get a sense of how postmodernism will affect librarianship.

Douglas Litowitz's *Postmodern Philosophy and Law* is one of the best recent studies of how postmodernism has affected legal theory. For the most part, Litowitz argues that postmodernism has had little direct effect, mainly because postmodernist philosophers have had little to say about legal theory. Much has to be derived from their works dealing with other issues. A further hindrance is the fact that postmodernism tends to focus on external critiques. That is, just as they would tend to ignore the statements made by lawyers and judges, postmodernists might ignore what librarians claim that they are doing, for example, when they resist creating a subject heading for "Looksism" or when they use "Mythology" to characterize the religious beliefs of non–Christian societies.

A further hindrance to the wide application of postmodernist thought in librarianship is its basic distrust of words and their meanings. While a modernist would insist that a "cigar" is always a "cigar," a postmodernist might say, yes, except when it is a Cuban cigar or a cheap "cheroot" or perhaps, in medical terminology, a "nicotine delivery system." A word is often open to a wide range of interpretations, depending on the perspective of the speaker. For example, Freud once insisted that "a cigar is sometimes only a cigar" (when he was smoking it, for example). A postmodernist would be deeply suspicious of the idea that a word could have only one meaning, while catalogers, on the other hand, depend on a commonly agreed meaning for certain words and phrases used as subject headings. A cataloger might resist for years changing "European war" to "World War I" even though the rest of the world had long ago abandoned the rather isolationist notion that this war was merely "European" in nature. Words often carry a political agenda. Whether you characterize someone as "pro-life" or "anti-abortion" does make a difference.

Our problem is that, if we decide to engage in a postmodernist critique of libraries, we will have to deal with both "good" postmodernists, including Foucault, Derrida, and de Man, and "bad" postmodernists, meaning Lacan, Baudrillard and several other theorists who have become associated with postmodernism. Some forms of postmodernism do not really advance us any further in trying to find a new direction for libraries. Some are just smoke-and-mirrors philosophizing, useless games with language, or dubious interpretations of behavior as somehow based on Freudian categories. In some ways Lacan is not far removed from some of the New Age religions in its use of mystical systems and bizarre theories.

I am not a fan of French-style philosophizing, or of navel-gazing or New Age therapies, all of which strike me as pretty much the same kind of stuff. But what is really interesting is to watch what happens when one of these gaseous works of philosophical and ideological mystification makes the mistake of running afoul of a solidly established ideology. Marie Balmary's *Psychoanalyzing Psychoanalysis* is just such a work, using Lacanian theories to deconstruct and psychoanalyze Freud himself. This book is actually a pretty good example of how far wrong postmodernism can go when it climbs out on the limb of Freudian interpretation. This book is worth examining at length.

Most of the reviews written about Marie Balmary's *Psychoanalyzing Psychoanalysis* were quite unflattering, attacking the author both for lapses in examining the historical facts of Freud's life and mistakes in how those facts were then interpreted. The evidence regarding Freud's father and the possibility of an earlier marriage is attacked on both the historical evidence and Balmary's interpretation, with the reviewers giving alternative explanations and readings of the evidence. Most reviewers pointedly refer to Balmary as an exponent of the Lacan school of French psychoanalysis, and associate her with the French feminist psychoanalysis of Luce Irigaray and others.

There is, as we all well know, a tendency in French critical theory to deal with the play and interplay of words in spite of (or in conflict with) the historical record. While American New Criticism advocated abandoning "history" in favor of interpretation, even these critics never imagined the lengths that French critics have gone to in recent years. The French not only killed "his/story" as a phallocentric enterprise, but they gutted it and now read its entrails as if it were a holy augury. For example, what we know about ancient Greek religion in general, and Dionysus in particular, has not really changed much in the last century, and Marcel Detienne's *Dionysos at Large* (1989) and similar books of French-Fried theory do not really advance us much beyond what we learned a century ago from Walter Pater's *Greek Studies.*

Balmary's book follows the French style pretty closely, concentrating on word play and the French lexicographic-endoscopic manner of entrail reading. The critics, however, seem to take Balmary's ideas seriously, in a very un–French way. Very interesting is the tendency of a number of reviewers to focus on Balmary's interpretation of the mushroom hunting expeditions led by Sigmund Freud and described by his son Martin in *Sigmund Freud: Man and Father* (1958). In his memoir, Martin Freud describes his father as leading the children on an expedition looking for a particular variety of savory mushroom, much enjoyed by the whole family. Balmary focuses on the very peculiar behavior of Dr. Freud in leading his children on this quest described by Balmary as "the mysterious capture of mushrooms" (page 39).

Balmary interprets several details of the mushroom hunts as especially peculiar, including Freud's word for the mushroom (Herrenpilze) which Balmary takes as signifying *Herr*: mister, master, lord, God. Why Freud chose to address the mushrooms as if they were little men, is significant to Balmary.

Of further interest is Freud's habit of tossing his hat over the mushrooms, as if he were capturing the mushroom at the point of its escape. Freud also describes the mushrooms as Steinpilze, or stone mushrooms, and associates this word with Freud's hobby of collecting and studying small statuary or "stone gentlemen" (page 40).

Balmary has constructed a mosaic of word associations that link Freud's mushroom expeditions with his feelings about his father, Jakob, and what she describes as the hidden "sexual fault of the father" (page 41). One reviewer humorously describes Freud's relationship with his father, Jakob, as a desire on Freud's part to eat the phalli of the paternal mushrooms — the shape of the mushrooms and Freud's description of them as "old men" leading to the obvious image of sexual abuse by the father, Jakob, and its transmission by veiled expressions in Freud's language and behavior.

All this may strike the average reader as rather bizarre. I would suggest, however, that there is an easier way to interpret this story and to deconstruct Dr. Freud's strange behavior and "the mysterious capture of mushrooms."

Almost unnoticed in this whole recitation and examination of Freud's mushroom hunting is the fact that Freud may have had another unrecognized motive for locating the savory "old men" mushrooms. In fact, going back to read Martin Freud's original memoir, we discover that Freud brought his children out into the forest to look for the savory mushrooms, but only indirectly. In his memoir Martin states that Freud sent the children out into the forest to look for a particular variety of toadstool, which was brightly colored, because, as Freud told his children, these toadstools grow near the hard-to-find savory Herrenpilze that they enjoyed eating. The children would look for the toadstools, and once they were located the children would then spread out from that location, searching for the savory mushrooms that, according to Dr. Freud, usually grew nearby.

There are, however, several problems with Martin Freud's description of this procedure. First, the brightly-colored toadstools that the children were instructed to search for are common in evergreen forests but they tend to grow in very specific types of soil. In fact, it is almost impossible to cultivate this variety of toadstool because it stubbornly refuses to grow in typical garden soils, preferring the soil adjacent to a specific species of evergreen tree or with a particular combination of trees. On the other hand, the tasty Herrenpilze (or Boletus) mushrooms that were supposedly the object of Freud's search tend also to be found in forests, but there is no reason to believe that they grow in the same type of soil. I will defer this question to the professional mycologists, but it seems very unlikely that you could easily locate the savory mushrooms by looking for the toadstools.

The question then is: Why would Freud direct his children to look for the toadstools if, in fact, he wanted them to find the Herrenpilze? And why did Freud go through the elaborate charade of throwing his hat over the savory Herrenpilz, as though they were little men?

The answer to these questions becomes much clearer if you consider the fact that the toadstools Dr. Freud had his children searching for are, in fact, a well-known hallucinogenic variety, common throughout Europe. There is every reason to believe that you could locate them in the Austrian Alps, where Freud and his children were hunting. The hallucinogenic toadstools were used in religious rituals throughout the world, and especially in Siberia where 18th century explorers first discovered and described their use. As a student of religious practices, Sigmund Freud could hardly claim ignorance of the use of these toadstools by the Eurasian shaman as part of his religious rituals. Given Dr. Freud's earlier experimentation with cocaine, it seems clear the he probably had an ulterior motive for locating the toadstools.

This explanation is given additional credibility by Freud's habit of throwing his hat over the mushrooms. In folklore, the toadstools are often portrayed as little men. In religious ritual, the shaman usually treats the toadstool as if it were a living being with human features and characteristics, including head and feet. For example, the shaman, when gathering toadstools, takes particular care in pulling the mushroom free from the ground so that no part of the mushroom is left behind. The shaman knows that if he is so clumsy as to break off the mushroom, later during his trance the mushroom spirits will complain about his leaving part of their "feet" behind. This tendency on the part of the shaman to regard the mushrooms as human would more readily account for Freud's using the word Herr to describe mushrooms than Balmary's alleged "Freudian" association of the mushrooms with his father.

Furthermore, Freud's hobby of collecting statuary could easily be part of a larger study of mushroom folklore, as many primitive statues reflect an ancient preoccupation with these hallucinogenic mushrooms. Freud's interest in the Steinpilze or Stone Gentlemen could easily have been part of his study of mushroom folklore. A comparison of Freud's habits and interests with the work of R. Gordon Wasson would be enlightening for most of Freud's biographers. Certainly a careful reading of Clark Heinrich's *Strange Fruit*, which describes his experiences with the Amanita mushroom, would be in order.

Thus we have three possible explanations for Dr. Freud's interest in mushrooms:

First, the historical explanation, that Freud enjoyed savory mushrooms and organized his children into expeditions for the purpose of locating them. This version fails to account for why he had them search for the hallucinogenic mushrooms which grow in areas somewhat different from where you could expect to find the savory variety of mushrooms. This explanation also fails to account for Dr. Freud's peculiar behavior with regard to the mushrooms.

Second, Balmary's theory that Freud's interest in mushrooms was part of a larger locus of psychological associations tied to the sexual "fault" of his father, Jakob Freud. While interesting in and of itself as a verbalization of the problem, this theory lends more smoke than fire to our understanding of Freud's mind.

Third, it seems likely that in the years following his unfortunate experimentation with cocaine, Freud may have secretly continued in his study of mind-altering drugs, including the hallucinogens. This theory has the advantage of explaining some of Dr. Freud's more bizarre bouts of behavior regarding the "Stone Gentlemen" or "Old Men" and his interest in small statuary. In retrospect, Freud's throwing his hat over the mushroom serves the function of a magician's hat — drawing the audience's attention away from the cards he has up his sleeve — so that in later years his children remember the action and focus on it, rather than on what they were really doing out there in the woods. I suspect that once the children located a growth area where toadstools were common, Dr. Freud simply kept track of where it was located and then had the children carry on with the search for the savory mushrooms which might or might not be somewhere nearby. It would be easy enough then to return to the location to gather the toadstools, and even to return year after year to this location.

It does seem rather odd to think of Freud using his children in this way to search for hallucinogenic mushrooms. This Freud seems almost Machiavellian in character, both clever and capable of improvisation and misdirection. This is perhaps a more realistic view of Freud than the paternal scion described by Martin Freud or the sexually-obsessed scholar described by Mary Balmary.

In several of the reviews critical of Balmary, she was described as an exponent of the Lacan school of French psychoanalysis and as part of French feminist psychoanalysis. Of course, once she is identified as an outsider to conventional Freudian thought, she becomes an easy target for the Freudian establishment. As much as I might sympathize with Balmary as the underdog in a decidedly one-sided fight, I doubt that the French school of psychoanalysis would be any less oppressive than the American school, if it ever came to power.

Some people might argue that Lacan was more reactionary than postmodernist, arguing for a return to Freud (in a sort of "Let Freud be Freud!" project) and to the original intent of Freud as "the founder" of psychoanalysis. It has been observed that revolutionaries are often reactionaries in disguise, like William Blake and Martin Luther King, Jr., in the sense that they wish to measure society by an ancient code of beliefs or return to a fabled Golden Age. It is possible, and even appropriate, to reform modernist institutions by using the language of modernism. Like libraries, civil rights are a modernist project.

Ultimately, as we move into the postmodern era, the arguments presented by critics of the established order (meaning critics of the American Library Association, of the Library of Congress, of Dewey, and of libraries as cultural institutions) will undergo changes in the way we approach this ongoing project. Because libraries are still very much a product of modernism, we will have to use the language of modernism, meaning words like "Truth / Justice / Equality," while working with the instruments of postmodernism, including deconstruction, to expose the inherent fallacies and inequalities that exist within the system.

I, for one, have no desire to see this postmodernist critique go down the path, exemplified by Balmary, of creating a fantastic pseudolanguage or mystical terminology. We can do without that. The issues of race and gender equity, civil rights, intellectual freedom, etc., can be defended in plain language, without following the extreme examples of Lacan and his followers.

REFERENCES

Balmary, Marie. *Psychoanalyzing Psychoanalysis: Freud and the Hidden Fault of the Father*. Baltimore: Johns Hopkins, 1982.

Detienne, Marcel. *Dionysos at Large*. Cambridge, MA: Harvard University Press, 1989.

Foucault, Michel. *The History of Sexuality*. New York: Pantheon, 1978.

Freud, Martin. *Sigmund Freud: Man and Father*. New York: Vanguard, 1958.

Heinrich, Clark. *Strange Fruit: Alchemy, Religion and Magical Foods, a Speculative History*. London: Boomsbury, 1994.

Litowitz, Douglas E. *Postmodern Philosophy and Law*. Lawrence, KS: University Press of Kansas, 1997.

May, Todd. *The Political Philosophy of Poststructuralist Anarchism*. University Park: Penn State Univ. Press, 1994.

Norris, Christopher. *What's Wrong with Postmodernism*. Baltimore: Johns Hopkins, 1990.

Pater, Walter. *Greek Studies*. London: Macmillan, 1925.

Chapter 6

Target ALA— The Culture War Moves to the Library

It's clear from the barrage of antilibrary propaganda being generated by James Dobson's Focus on the Family (FOF), that libraries are quickly becoming a battleground of the Culture War. Rather than targeting the large and powerful media giants who produce most of the "adult-oriented" material they object to, the Radical Right has decided to concentrate on an easy target: public libraries. Focus on the Family and the Family Research Council have, along with Pat Robertson's Christian Coalition, thrown their support behind a new library association called Family Friendly Libraries (FFL), which they hope will challenge the American Library Association as a professional organization that develops policies for libraries nationwide.

Some people will, no doubt, think it odd that a group of right-wing organizations who usually encourage censorship and support challenges to library materials now want to create a rival organization for libraries. But the reason for creating Family Friendly Libraries is clear. It is much easier to create procensorship library policies on a national level than try to censor on a case-by-case basis. These groups would prefer to gain political control over library boards, but failing that, they will use FFL's new procensorship "policies" as a stick to intimidate and harass library staffs.

For example, the founder of Family Friendly Libraries, Karen Jo Gounaud, used a "balanced-collection" argument to pressure the Fairfax County, Virginia, libraries to spend $1,100 on antigay fundamentalist literature. This should not, however, be taken as a sign that Focus on the Family or the Christian Coalition now support the idea of balanced collections. At the same time this was happening, in Anderson County, South Carolina, activists for the same right-wing organizations who support FFL were demanding that the book *Leaving the Fold: Testimonies of Former Fundamentalists* be removed from the shelves. This book, which was originally donated to the library by a local humanist group, has been the target of several right-wing challenges.

At the "Family Friendly Libraries" Conference held in 1995 in Cincinnati, the agenda of FFL was clearly stated by the titles of the meetings and by the affiliations of the speakers. These included meetings on such "problems" as "Homosexual Ideology Within the Library System," "Harmful Materials Available to Children," "Dealing with Anti-Family Boards of Trustees," and finally "And the Problem Is: The American Library Association." The speakers included representatives of Citizens for Community Values, the American Family Association, and the Christian Coalition. The focus of the meetings was clearly political, given that a great deal of emphasis was placed squarely on how to find and elect "Family Friendly" library board members.

And now, following on the heels of FOF's criticism of the American Library Association and Banned Books Week, the Family Research Council, in association with FOF, has decided that libraries are throwing away classic literature. A report by FRC entitled "Discarded Images: Selected Classics and American Libraries" suggests that library collections are being gutted at an alarming rate and that America's literary heritage is in peril.

Dobson's Focus on the Family, based in Colorado Springs, has already launched an attack on ALA through its *Citizen* newsletter. Both FOF and its research arm, the Family Research Council, have criticized "Banned Books Week" by announcing that there really is no "censorship" as such in this country since people who want books can buy them in bookstores. This claim seems fairly familiar, like the claim sometimes attributed to President Reagan, that there is no "hunger" in America because he saw empty tables at his favorite restaurant. Now that FOF has unmasked the American Library Association as "irresponsible" and "hysterical" for constantly crying wolf over censorship, the Family Research Council feels it can move on to attack libraries for failing to maintain collections of "classic" scholarship and works of cultural importance.

The FRC's survey of libraries, included as part of its report, is clearly designed to give the answer the researchers wanted. The FRC created a list of 100 books and sent a survey to libraries asking how many of the titles on the list were in each library's collection. Rather than ask solely for titles that were established classics, the survey included a list of lesser-known works by important authors, under the pretext that "if a library has *St. Ronan's Well*, it is rather likely that it has all of Scott's Waverley novels." The list of books includes such titles as Thackeray's *The Irish Sketch Book*, Thoreau's *The Maine Woods*, Chesterton's *Chaucer*, and Trollope's *Orley Farm*. I checked these titles in our own university library collection, which serves 6,000+ students and supports an M.A. program in English, and discovered that, although *The Maine Woods* was checked out in 1994 and *Chaucer* in 1992, *Orley Farm* was last checked out in 1988 and *St. Ronan's Well* in 1968. *The Good Soldier* was last checked out in 1981 and *The Irish*

Sketch Book, which is a fairly old and brittle copy, has apparently never been checked out, or at least not since it was rebound in 1980. Obviously, to suggest that a small or even a medium-sized public library should have these titles is absurd, when they get so little use in an academic library setting. Furthermore, it is an open question why any small public library would need a complete set of Scott's Waverley novels, let alone Thackeray's *Irish Sketch Book*. This survey is a classic example of the "straw man" fallacy; the results were fairly predictable based on the way the authors defined the question: "What makes a good library?"

The absurdity of this survey is further highlighted by the ignorance of its creators as to how modern libraries function. Generally speaking, many public libraries are cramped for space, often trying — as is our local public library here in Pittsburg, Kansas — to maintain itself in a very small Carnegie-era building. For example, until 1980, when the Pittsburg State University library moved to a much larger building, the librarians had to, quite literally, get rid of one book for each title that was added. This meant selecting several thousand books a year to be withdrawn. On some occasions the task became too daunting, and the library director took a hand in the process by getting rid of any books that were in poor condition or "didn't look right" on the shelf, or by getting rid of useless "popular fiction" by people like Steinbeck and Hemingway. Today, many public libraries are facing this same dilemma. They can't possibly serve their patrons effectively and, at the same time, try to act as warehouses for Western civilization. And, frankly, with the extensive use of interlibrary loan, it seems a rather strange idea for small or medium-sized libraries to try to function as storehouses.

The author of the FRC report "Discarded Images" also seems to think that libraries regularly get rid of books that are valuable collectibles. However, according to most book dealers, once a book has been stamped and processed for library use, it loses most of the value it could ever have as a collectible book. If libraries could sell withdrawn books for as little as $5 or $10 each, the library could afford to hire a staff person to withdraw these books and sell them. In fact, the vast majority of withdrawn books are virtually worthless, and libraries have trouble getting rid of them for 25 cents each, let alone the hundreds of dollars suggested by the author of "Discarded Images." This whole question is, of course, just another side issue — a feigned concern with "waste" from people who don't really care about libraries and simply want to smear librarians as "wasteful."

Many librarians may wonder why the Family Research Council bothered to do this survey. Its results were hardly a surprise, given the way it was designed. And yet it is clear, too, that, like many of the attacks in the ongoing culture wars, this may be an effort to divert attention away from the more serious issues facing libraries. In fact, libraries are facing an enormous number of very real problems in both access to information and fiscal constraints. Diverting scarce resources to buying a new set of the Waverley novels seems like the wrong answer to the wrong question.

In reality, libraries face the much larger question of what our role will be going into the next century. Do we focus on electronic access? Or do we, as this report suggests, focus on historical monographs? Do we create stronger networks for sharing resources? Or do we create core collections of books by Dead White Guys? Interestingly enough, the Family Research Council listed several dead Frenchmen, dead Germans, and even a few dead Romans, but no dead black men or women. It seems that in the FRC's version of "Judeo-Christian" civilization, Prescott's *History of the Conquest of Peru* makes the list of 100 important books, but *The Life and Times of Frederick Douglass* does not. A better question for a survey might be: How many libraries have both the Waverley novels *and* the novels of Toni Morrison? In an age of fiscal restraints, is it better to buy a copy of Morrison's *Beloved* or a reprint of Scott's *St. Ronan's Well*? An even more important question to librarians is, "In your library, which book is more likely to be read?"

It is also interesting to note that women authors are represented by less than 10 percent of the list, and the only women who make the list are novelists. After all, in the Victorian worldview, women are not intellectually suited to the rigors of rational argument. Also noteworthy is the fact that D.H. Lawrence and James Joyce do not make the list, probably because of their reputation as authors of "dirty" books. On the other hand, "dirty" authors like Rabelais, Zola, Hawthorne, and Molière do make the list. Evidently, the questionable authors of the past can be assimilated over time into the canon of Judeo-Christian culture. Although Chaucer did not make the list, a book about him that whitewashes his reputation and rehabilitates him as a "Christian" author does make the list as the only biography included. Apparently *The Canterbury Tales* is just too dirty (and funny) to recommend, except perhaps in bowdlerized editions. Although authors like Zola scandalized earlier generations, much of that is forgotten because censors have very short memories. The efforts to censor Lawrence and Joyce, however, are still fresh in their (and our) experience.

The Family Research Council and Focus on the Family devote a great deal of effort to trying to prove that the American Library Association has abandoned basic principles of librarianship that were considered vital in bygone years. This theme is echoed by right-wing critics, including Cal Thomas, whose editorial "Libraries Are Way Out in Left Field" laments that, in the old days, librarians "were free to acquire for their collections the best that has been thought and written." Today, of course, all we buy is trash, much like those trashy novels by Steinbeck and Hemingway that we used to buy back in the old days.

The clarion call of "quality" is one that we have heard over and over again during the last century. The attempt to identify and purchase quality is a primary goal of most acquisitions librarians. The problem is, of course, how you identify quality. In the case of the Family Research Council, quality is the exclusive product of Dead White Guys. Unfortunately, the call for quality often is a mask for prejudice, an effort to exclude a variety of minority groups from the public arena.

This is also true for libraries, and we can easily trace the thread of prejudice back to the time of Melvil Dewey. Dewey, perhaps more than anyone else, represents 19th century librarianship. Dewey, as founder of *Library Journal* and one of the founders of the American Library Association, is a pivotal figure in American librarianship. In his writings, one can easily find a variety of references to the importance of quality and discrimination on the part of librarians. This same concept is reflected in the membership requirements for the Lake Placid Club, established by Dewey, where it states, "No one shall be received as member or guest, against whom there is physical, moral, social or race objection," including "absolutely all consumptives, or other invalids." According to Dewey, just as we must carefully examine books for any defect that would prevent us from adding them to our libraries, people should be examined as to whether or not they are worthy to enter our society.

One might expect that, in some cases, both books and individuals might have "redeeming" qualities that would cause them to be added rather than rejected. In Dewey's world of Lake Placid, however, "It is found impracticable to make exceptions to Jews or others excluded, even when of unusual personal qualifications." Dewey's argument for exclusion is echoed today in calls for "quality" in the library. It is echoed, too, in the statement by Charles Donovan, senior policy advisor for the Family Research Council, when he says, "some things are so destructive to bonds of cohesion in a community or to its standards and laws that their rights to balance don't apply." And so, following the traditions of Dewey and the advice of Mr. Donovan, we should focus our efforts on buying multiple copies of Bill Bennett's *Book of Virtues* rather than anything that might be dangerous or harmful to society.

For example, a librarian could decide that she should avoid books that might cause some kind of "harm" as defined by Mr. Donovan. This means that you do not buy *The Anarchist Cookbook* because it contains information that might cause physical harm, if its readers are foolish enough to mix together the wrong chemicals. Most librarians would accept this as a reasonable standard. You could also argue that we should refuse to buy books like *The New Joy of Gay Sex* because some of the practices described in it might be harmful to your health. And libraries should also get rid of all their horror fiction, too, since children have a tendency to act out the things they read. And, of course, we really must get rid of all of our magazines that have advertisements for tobacco and alcohol products, given that so many thousands of people die from lung cancer and in alcohol-related accidents. This argument could easily be continued *ad infinitum*, so that the question becomes, "Where do you stop in your efforts to protect the public from harmful ideas, and who is to decide what is harmful?"

How we define "harm" can easily be taken to extremes, especially when it is applied by the habitual censor. Some censors might argue that even the Bible occasionally fails this test. Just recently the North Carolina-based *World* magazine attacked the International Bible Society and Zondervan Publishing House for planning to bring out an "inclusive language" version of the Bible. This translation, a variation of the NIV, the best-selling Bible among evangelicals in North America, would have replaced "man" with "people" or some other nongendered pronoun throughout the text. James Dobson and other evangelical religious leaders quickly condemned this version of the Bible as "misquoting God" and have prevented its publication in North America. It may be that they will further move to suppress its publication in Britain, where it is already available. The fundamentalists clearly see a "harm" in the way this version of the Bible might be used.

The problem here, whether we are talking about people or books, is that the censor's view of the world is exclusive, while the library selector should be inclusive. Applying a racist or regressive standard to book selection, whether that standard is labeled "Judeo-Christian" or "Family Friendly," is simply wrong. Libraries should strive to be inclusive rather than exclusive, and that means taking the risk that a particular book may cause some intangible spiritual "harm" or may offend some individual or group that objects to its content. The goals of a modern library should be quality and diversity in its collection. "Quality" should not be a code word for a homogenous "white-bread" type of collection which, as Milton might observe, neither offends the sensibilities of the powerful nor nourishes the souls of the weak.

REFERENCES

Maurina, Darrell Todd. "'Inclusive Language' Row Leads to Charge of Unethical Conduct." http://churchnet.ucsm.ac.uk/news/files2/inclusive.htm

Wiegand, Wayne A. *Irrepressible Reformer: A Biography of Melvil Dewey.* Chicago: ALA Editions, 1996.

Winell, Marlene. *Leaving the Fold.* Oakland, CA: New Harbinger, 1993.

Chapter 7

Freethought Materials in Libraries

A serious problem facing publishers of freethought material is that after the publisher has gone to the expense of editing, printing and marketing a book and after a library has decided to buy the book and gone to the time and expense of adding the book to the library's collection, the book is often cataloged in such a way that it is hard for library patrons to find. This is not necessarily the fault of individual libraries. During the last 20 years, libraries have come to rely heavily on sharing cataloging information, usually accessed through on-line systems like OCLC based in Dublin, Ohio. The Library of Congress (LC) has effectively promoted this sharing by setting up a system whereby publishers can provide the Library of Congress with author, title, and subject information about a book before the book is even published. Bookstores and libraries make decisions to buy books, especially potential bestsellers, sometimes before ink even touches paper. This system has been especially beneficial to large publishing houses.

The Library of Congress has for some years now done all its cataloging using an on-line system. By accessing information from on-line systems, many libraries save time and labor by simply copying the information provided by the Library of Congress. Because so many libraries copy Library of Congress cataloging, directly or indirectly, it is necessary for this reason to examine the way LC catalogs freethought materials to see if access to these materials can be improved. This problem is made even more urgent by the fact that public libraries often discard books that are not read, so that books which are hard to find usually end up being weeded from the library collection and discarded.

Recently, John Pope's *The Hellions*, a critique of television evangelists published by Prometheus Books, was cataloged by the Library of Congress with a "recommended" Dewey Classification of 200. The classification number 200 is the broadest possible number for religion and a book cataloged under this number should be about religion in general and not about any particular aspect, sect, or denomination of religion.

Interestingly enough, an OCLC participating library had already cataloged this same book under the Dewey Classification of 269.2, for Evangelists and Evangelism, so that the book would be placed on the shelf with other books by and about television evangelists. However, their original bibliographic record was "bumped" by the LC record, which has priority in the OCLC on-line cataloging system, so that most libraries will now no doubt use the "recommended" Dewey number assigned by the Library of Congress in cataloging their own copies of the book instead of the more appropriate number of 269.2 for evangelists. In effect, this book has been segregated into a section of the library well away from other books on the same topic. It is thus much less likely to be read by library patrons, and consequently much more likely to be discarded after a few years.

There is no reasonable justification for segregating freethought books in this way, especially when the books are easily identified as dealing with a subject much more specific than just "religion." Similarly, recently published books by M.T.W. Arnheim, George Albert Wells, J.M. Robertson, and Joseph Hoffman dealing with the historicity of Jesus Christ have been cataloged either in a general religion number, usually 200 or 201, or in the 230.09 range for theology, or even in 291.63 (a comparative religion number for "divinely inspired persons") rather than in the number 232.908, the correct Dewey number for the historicity of Christ. These books are effectively segregated away from books that deal with more traditional Christian views of Christ.

Even the bestseller books are often badly cataloged. A well known and controversial book by John Allegro was, even though it specifically dealt with the origins of Christianity, placed with books on the Dead Sea Scrolls. Similarly, the controversial *Holy Blood, Holy Grail*, a book that was publicly criticized by the Archbishop of Canterbury for suggesting that Christ may have had a wife and children, was recently cataloged with the recommended Dewey number 944 — the general number for French history! Furthermore, the two books on the same theme written by these same authors since the success of *Holy Blood, Holy Grail* have been cataloged under odd history numbers. *The Holy Place* is cataloged under 944.87 for the town of Rennes-le-Château, France (so that people who are interested in French local history can find it); and *The Messianic Legacy* is cataloged under 909, the general number for "world history" usually reserved for general histories of the world (the British Library was more generous, putting the book under 291.9 for "Sects and reform movements"). The question is, Why are these books being cataloged in such a bizarre fashion?

Because of its size, the catalogers at the Library of Congress are specialized in the material they deal with. There are "history" catalogers, "literature" catalogers, "science" catalogers, et al. The source of the problem seems to be that freethought books are usually cataloged by the "religion and philosophy" catalogers at the Library of Congress. Based on the minimal level of subject access that these catalogers usually provide, it would seem that they are, at best, uninterested in ideas expressed in freethought books.

The attitude of indifference is, at least, better than the outright hostility displayed by some catalogers over the years at some of our largest research libraries. Some years ago these librarians often cataloged books by the controversial ex-priest Joseph McCabe as "fiction" or cataloged them without any subject headings at all. McCabe was a popular author in the first half of this century who wrote "scandalous" books about religion and what goes on in various religious orders. He was an obvious target for people who disapproved of his ideas.

Controversial books like *Holy Blood, Holy Grail, The Sacred Mushroom and the Cross*, or even the recent book, Stephen Michaud's *If You Love Me, You Will Do My Will*, are almost impossible to find in the library unless you know the author or title. The latter book, which tends to cast a lurid light on the way some churches solicit funds, is cataloged under PROBATE LAW AND PRACTICE—TEXAS. Ultimately these books remain viable as a part of the library collection only as long as people use word-of-mouth to keep them viable. A similar book that criticized the Mormon church would almost certainly have included the subject heading MORMON CHURCH—CONTROVERSIAL LITERATURE. In fact, the catalogers at the Library of Congress appear to be much more efficient in cataloging books critical of the Mormon church than they are in cataloging books critical of "mainstream" churches.

Because most of these "religion" catalogers are, at best, uninterested in freethought, many of the books that they catalog tend to receive little in the way of subject access. In terms of research, a comparison of how these same freethought books have been cataloged by the Hennepin County Library in Minnetonka, Minnesota, whose practices regarding the use of subject headings are much more progressive than LC's, would show just how bizarre some of the Library of Congress practices are.

1. The Library of Congress needs to set a policy of not dumping freethought books into the general number 200 or 201. Some helpful changes were made in the Dewey schedule in 1993, but many freethought books are still segregated in 211, well away from the 230–270 books that they critique. Similarly, books that deal with "New Age" religious ideas should not be dumped into 291 just to avoid offending the devout. Books that deal with the historicity of Christ should be cataloged under the appropriate number, 232.908, and have the subject heading JESUS CHRIST—HISTORICITY.

2. When a publisher indicates in the CIP process that his or her book deals with freethought, this book should automatically be routed to catalogers other than the "religion" catalogers. Some publishers, like Prometheus Press, should automatically have their books routed to areas other than "religion."

3. The Library of Congress needs to be more sensitive to the way controversial literature is cataloged. This is true not only of religious material, but also of politically controversial books. For example, when you walk into a library and find that a book on the shootings at Kent State is cataloged with the subject heading EDUCATION—OHIO or when the Kerner Commission report on civil disorder published in 1968 is virtually impossible to find, even though your library has several editions and you know that popular columnist Tom Wicker wrote the introduction to the copy you saw in the bookstore — when these kinds of problems take place, then you know that something is seriously wrong.

In general, books that represent other than mainstream views are often not taken seriously, if not actively miscataloged. This is a practice that should not be encouraged, let alone aided and abetted, by the Library of Congress. Clearly, an institution the size of LC has many serious problems that get a higher priority than how to catalog freethought materials. Yet it seems to me that some level of equity can be reached in the way LC regards traditional and nontraditional beliefs, including freethought, with very little additional effort.

Some librarians might argue that freethought books are not very popular and don't deserve any "special" attention. I would have to admit that some freethought books are dull. However, few would reach the level of dullness achieved by many fundamentalist authors. On the contrary, freethought books can circulate well, where they are given sufficient subject access. In our library *The Book Your Church Doesn't Want You to Read* (1993) is one of the most popular books we own. This book is just one of several freethought titles that we have trouble keeping on the shelf. If freethought books don't circulate well in your library, it may say a lot more about how these books have been cataloged than about the general quality of freethought books.

REFERENCES

Baigent, Michael, Richard Leigh, and Henry Lincoln. *Holy Blood, Holy Grail.* New York: Delacourte, 1982.

____, ____, and ____. *Messianic Legacy.* New York: Henry Holt, 1987.

Leedom, Tim C., ed. *The Book Your Church Doesn't Want You to Read.* Dubuque, IA: Kendall/Hunt, 1993.

Michaud, Stephen G., and Hugh Aynesworth. *If You Love Me, You Will Do My Will.* New York: New American Library, 1991.

Pope, John. *The Hellions.* Amherst, NY: Prometheus, 1987.

Robertson, J.M. *Pagan Christs: Studies in Comparative Hierology.* London: Watts, 1911.

Chapter 8

Women's Studies
in the University

There has been during the past few years a continuing assault (or "backlash") against women's studies as a part of higher education. This assault has just recently started to make itself felt in the smaller regional universities, many of whom have only recently begun to look at women's studies as a legitimate topic for scholarship. It is also important to understand this backlash in the larger context of what is going on in higher education in America, as part of a general reaction against multicultural education. Much of this reaction is driven by the so-called "Institute for Advanced Conservative Studies" (meaning the followers of Rush Limbaugh) and by ultraconservative religious and political organizations, including the Intercollegiate Studies Institute.

The political agenda of ISI and these other organizations is very clear. Most of these organizations see the advancement of women and of minority cultures as a direct threat to conservative political institutions, and they would like to see internecine warfare break out between these groups and more traditional programs in higher education. The ISI gives away free subscriptions to its campus newspaper and to its journal *The Intercollegiate Review*, which many faculty all over the country receive. Anyone who reads a copy of ISI's campus newspaper can see that its primary purpose is to attack political correctness in general and women's studies and multicultural education in particular. Although ISI's focus is on institutions like Duke University, where a number of avant-garde programs have been instituted, they sometimes also go after the small fry.

For example, the spring 1998 issue of ISI's *Campus* includes several articles attacking affirmative action, a report on the newspaper's "1998 Campus Outrage Awards" (which focuses on a fairly implausible story about a faculty member denied tenure for teaching Shakespeare), and its regular "Campus Wire," which includes the usual hodgepodge of attacks on things like the distribution of condoms, courses on gender studies, various transgressions by "radical" student organizations, and so on. This issue of *Campus* also includes a book review of (imagine that!) Christopher Ruddy's *The Strange Death of Vincent Foster* (1997) and a review of Michael Lewis's *Poisoning the Ivy: The Seven Deadly Sins and Other Vices of Higher*

Education in America (1997). I imagine many academics would agree with some, if not all, of the criticisms summarized in the review of *Poisoning the Ivy*, but I would also suggest that a glowing review of the Ruddy book is prima facie evidence of the far-rightward lean of this newspaper. Like most newspapers that are published to advance a particular agenda, *Campus* is an interesting mix of hearsay and attack journalism, not unlike the fare found in *Reader's Digest*.

In spite of the criticism of multicultural studies coming from ISI and other organizations, there is good reason for having courses that deal with issues of race, sexual orientation and sexual or artistic expression. Furthermore, it is important to bring these courses together under one banner. There is an inherent strength to be gained when a group of related though somewhat diverse courses can be brought together and considered as part of a unit. They are then given greater legitimacy within the institution and can be considered as a group in planning for the future of the university.

Some people may question whether we really need something called "multicultural" education. That is, do we really need courses whose purpose is to make us more sensitive to other races and cultures? Although some people might disagree, I think we need all the help we can get. On the larger scale we have recently had a rash of burnings of black churches in this country. On a smaller scale, in our town I recently volunteered to help at a day camp for our local Boy Scouts at the park where I saw racism firsthand. While a group of boys were standing around the BB-gun shooting range, several Scouts spontaneously broke out into song. The song seemed fairly innocuous, until they got to the line "shot a nigger in '59" at which point one of the mothers shut them up. The fact that one of the volunteers who was helping with the BB-gun range was a black soldier with the National Guard didn't seem to register with these kids.

Although some people may feel that this falls into the same category as the constitutionally protected right to catcall and whistle at female students, I suspect that most of us realize that this is really just the tip of the iceberg. There is in fact a deeply entrenched racism in most, if not all, of our communities that many faculty see reflected in the ideas of their students. Pretending that it doesn't exist or that it really isn't that significant may be the easy and comfortable way out, but I feel that a university has a responsibility to educate the people in the local community in more than just readin', writin' and cipherin'.

Critics often attack gender and minority studies on the basis that these courses are not academic enough. This is a fairly common ploy on the part of traditional academics who want to cut or curtail gender and minority studies. First, critics typically try to claim that gender and minority studies are passing fads. The only answer I can make to this is, if it is a fad, it is taking a hell of a long time to pass! Women's studies, in particular, has been a part of higher education for at least the last 30 years, and there are no signs that it shows any abatement. Although ISI and other conservative think tanks would like to see it pass and have been attacking its legitimacy for years, it seems to keep going.

Since the material dealt with in women's studies as an area of intellectual inquiry hasn't been around for a few centuries or so, it seems unfair to question, as some do, its "academic heritage." Most people would suggest Mary Wollstonecraft's *The Vindication of the Rights of Women* (1792) as a starting point for what has become women's studies. Granted that it is not as hoary with age as math or geography, it should be granted too, that at least there are new horizons in this field, whereas in many disciplines there is very little scholarship going on that has much relevance to our students' lives. And many disciplines seem to be badly ossified and preoccupied with little more than discovering new techniques for teaching and new ways to use computers.

This is certainly the case here at Pittsburg State University. Going through back issues of the *Graduate School Bulletin*, I saw a good deal of research and publication going on in several departments dealing with "gender" issues. In terms of books being published, Julie Allison's book *Rape, the Misunderstood Crime* was published recently by Sage, and the University of Missouri Press published Dr. Kathleen De Grave's *Swindler, Spy, Rebel: The Confidence Woman in Nineteenth Century America*. It seems ironic that, considering the amount of real scholarship going on in gender studies on this campus, compared with the lackluster scholarly output of some departments in the so-called "hard" sciences, that faculty members choose to attack gender studies as being not sufficiently "academic."

Second, conservative faculty members often criticize the tendency of faculty who teach gender studies (though not necessarily on this campus — after all, they wouldn't want to actually try to document this) to go off on "tangents" and to emphasize the "victim" status of women. It seems an easy target to stand in the doorway and point out what is or is not tangential to the subject.

It would be easy to cite national statistics on the average wages earned by women and minorities, when compared with white males, but we might be encroaching too far into the domain of the hard sciences in using this type of argument. As far as women's "victim" status is concerned, I know of a faculty member on our campus who spends a good deal of time each semester complaining about how his ex-wife treated him. No one here seems concerned about his going off on this tangent, and, as far as I know, no one questions his preoccupation with his own "victim" status. On the other hand, some women students have a good deal of experience as victims, as survivors of frat parties might testify. I think that, nationwide, many white male faculty and department chairs are overly concerned with protecting their right to sexually harass their female students.

Third, a favorite point of attack is to question whether gender and women's studies are *really* academic disciplines. There is a tendency to question these topics as if they were just a bunch of touchy-feely therapy sessions.

These are serious matters, or they turn serious when it comes time to grant tenure and promotion to the faculty who teach these classes.

Questions about methodology, standards of scholarship, etc., are serious issues, and these critics make some interesting points. Because gender studies is generally considered to be a part of the social sciences, it is subject to much the same questions about methodology and standards of scholarship that persist within the social sciences generally. Sloppy scholarship should not be defended because of the point of view of the scholar.

Some conservative faculty profess to be honestly concerned about the fact that most of the students who take women's studies courses are women. Imagine that! How could this come to pass, that fewer men than women are interested in taking these courses? We could, of course, look into why more men are not taking these courses, but it is much easier simply to discontinue the courses — after all, if men are not taking the courses, there must be something wrong with the courses. And, of course, while we are at it, perhaps we should think about discontinuing the women's basketball program since there are no men on the team.

Ultimately, a university should take responsibility for its prejudices and work to try to move women and minorities into a role of greater equality in the academy. This may mean doing more than just trying to increase the percentage of women in science and technology. It may mean seriously rethinking the whole academic experience to figure out what we are doing and why we are doing it.

REFERENCES

Allison, Julie A., and Lawrence Wrightsman. *Rape: The Misunderstood Crime.* Newbury Park, CA: Sage, 1993.

De Grave, Kathleen R. *Swindler, Spy, Rebel: The Confidence Woman in Nineteenth Century America.* Columbia: University of Missouri Press, 1995.

Chapter 9

Intellectual Freedom
vs. Intellectual Property

The advent of the computer and the so-called information society has led to a rapid change in the way we look at information and ideas. Not only information, but ideas themselves have become property. Once it was only the peculiar grouping of words that was protected by copyright, while the realm of scientific inventions and technological developments were protected by patents. But now the whole business has been drawn together as "intellectual property" and has to be treated, at least in the courts, as related. At the same time intellectual property have become new buzz words in corporations, especially technology companies, biotech firms, and any company that deals with the media. Now that they know that words have a dollar value, they are becoming obsessed with exploiting those words, much like a timber company that has discovered an old growth forest in its backyard.

To understand what this means, and its implications for issues like intellectual freedom, we first need to understand corporate culture. Over the centuries, human society has developed in the sense of becoming more complex, but most of the basic behaviors remain the same. Scholars have studied corporate culture for most of this century, but they really don't seem to be much closer to understanding it, and cartoons like *Dilbert*, *Blondie* or even *Beetle Bailey* seem to have a better grasp of the problems of human behavior, intuitively, than the philosophical descendants of Frederick Taylor with his idea of "scientific management."

Corporations rise and fall based on the way they develop one or more of four basic functions. A growing corporation has learned either (1) how to exploit natural resources more cheaply, (2) how to manufacture a product more efficiently, (3) how to exploit workers more completely, or (4) how to exploit markets more thoroughly. A corporate empire rises and falls depending on how well it accomplishes one or more of these functions, compared with competing companies. For example, a company that has learned how to make dog food for about half of what it costs its competitors to make dog food can effectively dominate the market for dog food. This is assuming, of course, that dogs actually *like* this new and cheaper kind of dog food.

123

A company can grow and expand based on doing one or more of these functions well. This is the idea behind companies' trying to discover and develop their "core" business (yes, some companies are so dumb that they forget what their core business is and have to try to find it again). But just because a company is successful does not mean that the internal organization of this company is scientific, rational, humane or efficient. In fact, a number of corporations have risen to prominence that were run by executives who were complete loonies (like, for example, Howard Hughes), and the corporate culture reflected their personal looniness. The idea that financial success reflects some form of spiritual "goodness" is a holdover from the old Protestant work ethic. Even today we seem to automatically assume that a successful company owes its success to better management techniques, when in fact the company may simply have a solid grasp on one or more of the four basic functions of resources, production, personnel, and markets.

A successful company is not necessarily a company that makes any sense in the way it is run. As long as a company does its "core" function well, the rest of the company is mostly irrelevant, even if the rest of the company functions like a bunch of chimps playing with word processors trying to write mission statements. This is one of the more obvious messages of the *Dilbert* cartoons. Or, to put it another way, as long as the frontline workers are doing their jobs with a reasonable level of competence, the efforts of the managerial staff are mostly irrelevant. The Japanese seem to have figured this out a long time ago, as the typical Japanese corporation functions with no more than three or four levels of middle managers, unlike American corporations which often have as many as twelve levels.

Although you might allow that a company that controls a cheap natural resource, or a company that has effectively cornered the market on a product, could continue to prosper in spite of its management, it is perhaps harder to see how a company could prosper that depends on exploiting the workers, while at the same time having a management system that is inefficient, or even downright bizarre. This is especially true of service companies, since the prosperity of the corporation depends on providing a personal service to customers. Upon reflection, I think it's easy to see that, as long as the frontline workers, those who deal directly with the customers, function in an efficient manner, the actions of the management behind the scenes are largely irrelevant to the success of the enterprise.

The best example of this idea is to look at the history of warfare. The rise and fall of nations depends largely on their ability to field an effective armed force. In spite of the importance of military power to the survival of a society, we really don't understand very much about warfare, and military science still exists pretty much in the dark ages in terms of understanding what elements lead to defeat or victory on a battlefield. The factors involved are almost too varied to be measurable, let alone predictable. In terms of history, we know that the Romans were able to maintain their empire, largely because of the effectiveness of the Roman legions. They succeeded in spite of having emperors who were inefficient, lazy, unstable, or out-and-out insane. They also succeeded in spite of a government bureaucracy back in Rome that was thoroughly corrupt and inefficient. We should, of course, keep in mind that the enemies of Rome (like, for example, the Egyptians) were typically even more corrupt and inefficient than the Romans.

Victories in battle can often be attributed to greater numbers, better weapons, or better position on the field. An effective field commander can also make a real difference in the outcome of a battle. This fact is shown historically by the battles of Waterloo and Gettysburg, where the lack of a particular field officer directly affected the outcome of the war. However, the difference between victory and defeat is rarely influenced by the "management style" of the staff at the military headquarters. All other things being equal, the competence of the headquarters staff might affect the outcome of a battle; but the outcome is more likely to depend on the terrain, the weather, or what the soldiers had to eat that morning. The headquarters staff is only relevant to the extent that it probably had some influence on what the soldiers had for breakfast.

This principle carries over into the business world, and into the world of nonprofit organizations, including schools, hospitals and libraries. To some extent, nonprofit organizations are even less vulnerable to the incompetent manager than a for-profit business. You rarely hear of a library being closed because of incompetent management.

Most of my own experience has been working in civil service and higher education, so some people might be skeptical of my opinions about how corporations function. I would argue that there are really more similarities than differences, especially in recent years as universities have been trying more and more to emulate how things are done in the corporate world. For example, while a corporation has a board of directors, a university has to answer to a board of trustees. I would further argue that these boards of trustees are usually just as clueless about what is going on as the typical board of directors (or the typical library board). The members of a board of directors usually owe their position to a special relationship with the chief executive, and they are drawn from positions outside the organization they pretend to "direct." Most directors have no personal knowledge of how the enterprise on whose board they serve functions. They are totally dependent for information on the chief executive or the organization's staff; and the board members, in virtually all situations, are easily led around by the nose. In fact, many organizations go out of their way to avoid putting people on the board who might know something about the business that they supposedly run.

Similarly, many of the people who serve on the board of trustees for a university have a background in business rather than government or the non-profit sector, so that even their general background is not well suited to making good judgments about what the university is doing, or should be doing. To make matters worse, there is always someone, working for the university, who tries to curry favor with the board by bringing up issues that have been in the news as a new "business" trend. This is how we got "outsourcing" foisted off on us. This is how we got "Goals 2000" and a host of other "policy initiatives"—a phrase that makes educators cringe every time they hear it.

One consequence of the general cluelessness of governing boards is that many universities are now taking up the issue of intellectual property. This issue has been a concern with corporations, especially those companies that are heavily involved in research and development. Much of their research involves products that are worth literally millions of dollars; obviously these companies have to have some mechanism in place to keep that research from simply walking out the door when a researcher leaves for another job.

On the other hand, most of the research and publication that takes place in the university does not, unfortunately, have a high dollar value. A scholarly book that sells relatively well might earn $500 to $1000 in royalties in its first good year. It certainly never returns the investment of time and effort put out by the author, and very few "independent" scholars are able to make a decent living from their work. Few faculty members outside of science and technology make much money for the time they invest in research and scholarship.

At the same time, the people on the board of trustees tend to view the faculty of the university as being pretty much like the people who work for them in their factories or their fast-food restaurants. It's not hard to understand, then, why they view faculty as being in a state of indentured servitude with respect to the board. Questions of intellectual freedom are alien to their way of thinking. And so the typical trustee might be likely to believe that the university "owns" any sort of "intellectual property" that a faculty member might produce.

Although most universities claim to support research and scholarly activity, it is hard to imagine a policy more likely to have exactly the opposite effect. Why would any faculty member undertake the additional burden of research and scholarship, knowing that the results of that work will be summarily appropriated by the university? I can't imagine a similar policy being promoted anywhere outside of a communist society.

In cases where the university provides special financial support or equipment, an argument might be made that the university should share in any financial gains that come from that research. But when we are talking about work done by faculty in the evenings or on weekends, and without any special support from the university, it seems ludicrous for the university to claim ownership of this work.

In some cases, the university tries to distinguish between the scholarly activity of particular faculty members in terms of whether or not the intellectual property they create is within or outside their area of professional expertise. In other words, if a physics professor writes a novel, that novel is not related to his duties teaching physics. But if an English professor writes a novel, the novel would become the property of the university. I'm not sure what they would do with someone like Isaac Asimov, who wrote science fiction. The lawyers should really love this! It creates meaningless distinctions. If faculty are going to be treated as slaves, they should all be slaves equally.

Some universities also seem to think that they have ownership rights of intellectual property because they have "supported" the faculty member in some vague undetermined way. As the author of several manuscripts, I should ask: Is the university going to call publishers for me? Is the university going to provide me with a secretary to help in typing up manuscripts? Is the university going to act as my literary agent? The university may think that it has "supported" my research, but aside from letting me use an old IBM microcomputer in the evenings, I am hard pressed to know how it has supported my research. It has provided little or nothing in the way of financial support beyond the access to computers and printers, the same access it provides to students for free. I suspect that, in fact, the university only plans to come into the picture *after* all the real work is done and then lay claim to all the copyrights and royalties that result from my efforts.

In fact, many faculty have already been told by their publishers and by other colleagues in publishing that most publishers are *not* going to bother with trying to deal with the university bureaucracy in acquiring manuscripts for publication. These publishers will simply go elsewhere. In this way a university's claim to "ownership" of intellectual property will become a serious handicap to the faculty member in trying to get scholarly works published.

In some cases, the universities offer to transfer the copyrights back to the faculty member, once they have examined the work and determined that it has no real commercial value. Of course, the university typically reserves the right to use this work, without payment, if it is determined later that they were wrong and that the work does have a value. In fact, universities that control a university press could conceivably simply reprint a faculty member's writing without his or her consent.

If universities nationwide tried to enforce control over intellectual property, it would mean the death of intellectual freedom in this country. By asserting these vague "property" rights, the universities are also asserting control over this property, which includes the power to suppress any writings they don't like. Our much vaunted "Intellectual Freedom" won't mean much if the university asserts control of our words and ideas as its "property" to do with as it pleases.

What happens if a university decides to assert its property rights over the speeches and writings of a social critic like Noam Chomsky? Suddenly there is enormous temptation for the university trustees to try to "moderate" or "influence" or "filter" Professor Chomsky's more political ideas. And there are people who would encourage them to do just that.

In a recent newspaper editorial entitled "Trustees: From Scapegoats to Potential Heroes," conservative columnist Ben Wattenberg asserts that boards of trustees can, on a nationwide basis, be a strong force for correcting the "liberal bias" of the classroom. Wattenberg suggests that trustees can exercise greater control over wayward faculty. Certainly, if trustees assert their property rights to all the "intellectual properties" produced by the faculty, including their classroom lectures, then they have legal authority and control over everything that a faculty member says or writes.

Not only that, when a university asserts these types of property rights, it virtually assures that the best and brightest of the faculty at the institution will move on to other institutions rather than risk losing control over their own words and ideas. The only faculty who will stay at this type of university will be those who aren't particularly worried about having their ideas appropriated, because they don't have any. Having nothing to lose, they should feel comfortable in this environment.

What is even more insulting about this type of policy is that it unfairly singles out faculty who produce intellectual property, while ignoring faculty who do other kinds of business. At the university where I work, there are a number of faculty who run small businesses "on the side"— a faculty member who teaches in technology has a small auto shop, another faculty member builds houses. A professor in psychology does some counseling, another is a paid "expert witness" in the court system. These people will not be affected by this policy because they would simply stop working if the university tries to take their income. The faculty who create "intellectual property" are thus unfairly singled out by this type of policy.

Some people may claim that faculty are rewarded for research and publication through pay increases allotted through our so-called merit system. Our merit system is, of course, another carryover from the business world, and it, too, typically functions in a wholly irrational manner. The theory is, of course, that you recognize and reward merit by giving larger pay increases to "productive" faculty. Of course, when it comes time to recognize who the productive faculty are, objective measures are rarely ever used to separate the wheat from the chaff.

My own experience with the merit system, both in civil service and in education, has not been a happy one. In most cases the evaluation system is not very effective in terms of identifying areas where someone can seek to improve his or her performance, which is the most common rationale used for implementing this system. Rather, merit appraisal systems quickly degenerate into a political game played by the bosses, at the expense of frontline employees.

For example, I know of one case where a supervisor convinced upper management to hire a "star" engineer at an exorbitant salary. It turned out later that this engineer was less than stellar in his abilities; but, in spite of what was obvious to everyone else, the supervisor regularly gave the engineer the highest possible raises and merit evaluations. After all, to give the engineer a lower evaluation would be the same thing as admitting to upper management that the supervisor had made a mistake in hiring this engineer at such a high salary in the first place. Thus, the supervisor manipulated the merit evaluation to prove to his superiors that he himself was doing his job right.

I'm sure that virtually everyone who has worked with a merit system can give equally bizarre examples of how dysfunctional the merit system can be. A friend told me how, on one occasion, his supervisor gave his team the same rank in merit that was given to a team of misfits run by a chronic alcoholic who regularly fell asleep at his desk. Similarly, this same supervisor regularly gave the highest possible evaluation to a team led by a worker who rarely put in more than 20 hours a week on the job, mainly because he spent so much time on the other side of town working with some rental properties that he owned. It's hard to imagine which you would find more humiliating, being lumped in with the incompetent or being topped by the usually absent, part-time landlord. In both cases the merit ranking was based on a political agenda, rather than on any real merit.

In the first case, the alcoholic's team was "bumped up" in merit in order to avoid a confrontation with the poor slobs who had to work with him. The alcoholic was himself politically "connected" and couldn't be fired, and because he was a manager he needed someone to manage. In the second case the absentee landlord was part of a team that, during a recent reorganization, was placed under the supervisor's control. The absentee landlord was widely believed, before the reorganization, to be in line for a promotion to supervisor when his boss retired. This promotion never materialized and his team was merged under this supervisor. So his new boss gave him high merit evaluations as a consolation prize — and because an open rebellion might cost him his own promotion, which translated into about $20,000 a year. In both cases the merit system was used by the supervisor to advance himself and his own personal agenda.

The only management goal that merit systems accomplish is the creation of a sense of divisiveness among the employees. Although it was originally created as a system of rewards for "motivating" workers, the merit system is more often part of a larger political game being played by managers, as various individuals and teams compete (or not) for the prize of recognition and raises. The result of the game depends on whether the manager is bucking for promotion and empire-building, or whether he is actively avoiding recognition and promotion, like the concentration camp officer in the play *The Man in the Glass Booth*. In this story, the officer avoids promotion because it means getting closer to Hitler, and (in his view) being closer to Hitler means being closer to the Eastern Front. The politics of management have an irrationality all their own.

Like the so-called merit system, the current interest in controlling intellectual property is a carryover from the corporate world that doesn't work very well and often has a dampening effect on innovation and creativity. It discourages the more productive workers and creates a complex political game that harms the overall goals of the organization, by diverting time and resources that could better be spent making a better dog food.

REFERENCES

Shaw, Robert. *The Man in the Glass Booth*. New York: Harcourt, Brace & World, 1967.

Wattenberg, Ben. "Trustees: From Scapegoats to Potential Heroes" [syndicated editorial] April 20, 1997.

Chapter 10

Outsourcing the Public Library: The "Chains" of Librarianship

Many librarians have followed the "outsourcing" fiasco in Hawaii, which recently led to the firing of state librarian Bart Kane and lawsuits being filed against each other by Baker & Taylor and the State of Hawaii. But this episode has overshadowed outsourcing projects in other states, including in some cases the complete outsourcing of *all* library functions. It appears to many of us that this is a trend that is simply not going to go away. In fact, the only development that could conceivably tend to counter this one would be a growing respect (and self-regard) for libraries, including a greater sense of librarianship as a profession. Given the fact that this seems more and more unlikely, especially as our professional organization, the American Library Association, and its various roundtables seem to stumble over each other in an effort to curry favor with book vendors, we can probably look forward to more outsourcing in the future, rather than less.

Anyone who would dispute this should look carefully at the March 1998 issue of *American Libraries*. In addition to the continuing debate over outsourcing in the "Reader Forum," this issue includes an article entitled "What If You Ran Your Library Like a Bookstore?" Essentially, this article compares chain bookstores with libraries and describes how bookstores are more cost-effective. Most of these savings are achieved by cutting out salaries of the librarians and library assistants, while requiring that library aides do more reference work with patrons. This article is followed by "The Good Professional: A New Vision" which clearly makes the point that librarians are being replaced by paraprofessionals, and so we need to concentrate on making sure that the remaining professional librarians have a wide range of skills, from cataloging to personnel management. The library of the future will, of course, rely on the judicious use of outsourcing.

Given that outsourcing is likely to grow more common in the future, we need to give thought to what that means for the communities we serve. In all likelihood we will see book jobbers becoming more active as purveyors of "management services" for libraries. In some cases they will provide everything except the library building itself, including the library staff, the catalog, and for new branch libraries an "opening day" collection.

On the downside, these corporate "chain" libraries will probably tend to reflect to a large extent the corporate biases of their culture. Don't look for a chain library to initiate a subscription to "radical" publications like *The Nation*, and chain libraries are unlikely to subscribe to *Teamster* or other pro-union publications. For the most part, these chain libraries will do little more than carry the books published by big establishment publishers, inoffensive books by smaller specialized presses (look for a new version of *What Color Is Your Parachute* every few years), and the fewest possible reference titles. They are unlikely to buy anything by South End, Seven Stories, See Sharp, Cleis, or any of the more radical presses, except perhaps in a few large communities where there is already a fairly well established demand for such material.

As happens with other privatized services, the workers in a corporate "chain" library are likely to put more emphasis on following the "rules" than on achieving the goals of the library. That means that the ideals of public service will be largely supplanted by rules like "Don't antagonize the patron," "Don't waive fines without your supervisor's permission," and "Don't accept gift books." Some of these rules will simply reflect the codification of established library practices, but others will frequently run counter to the overall goal of library service, which will already have been supplanted by the golden rule of "Make a Profit!" After all, these library management services promise contractually to provide a city with a certain level of service at a fixed price; they then make their profit based on how they can cut corners on what it costs them to provide these services. Their goal is, first, to make money.

When compared with the libraries that exist in large urban communities, the chain library will always fall short, particularly in the area of collection development. The focus of the chain libraries will be on negotiating price breaks with the large publishing houses, not with finding the best sources of information. Granted that "best" is a qualitative term that is not easily measured, it is the fact of not being easily measured that makes it a likely candidate for extinction. For the corporate chain, those things that cannot be measured in terms of "units of service provided" are likely to be ignored.

In terms of defending "intellectual freedom" the chain library will almost certainly make whatever gestures are necessary to mollify critics. Every library will have one token copy each of *Daddy's Roommate* and *Heather Has Two Mommies*. And the chain libraries will have a large law firm in New York on a hefty retainer to defend to the death the right of the chain libraries to lend *Huck Finn* and *For Whom the Bell Tolls*, no matter how many people complain and demand that they be withdrawn from the collection.

On the other hand, chain libraries are unlikely to order many copies of *Best Gay Erotica* or *Best Lesbian Erotica*, and they are even less likely to loan copies of the video *The Tin Drum* without a proof of age or a parental permission statement, signed in triplicate. They will, of course, avoid books critical of particular political figures, like Pat Robertson and Dr. James Dobson, not to mention other groups and organizations, like the Moonies, Focus on the Family, and the Christian Coalition, all of which have political influence and are capable of creating an organized campaign against chain libraries, spread across several states. Chain libraries will not be on the front line of censorship battles, except in a few high-profile cases where they fail to retreat fast enough to suit the local censors.

In terms of lost income, the big losers will, of course, be the small and medium-sized presses and the scholarly presses, most of whom will be unable to provide chain libraries with the kind of discounts they need to remain profitable. The winners will be the megacorporation publishing establishment and the large Time-Warner–type media empires, along with various automation providers.

In terms of communities, the larger cities have the most to lose by the rise of the corporate chain libraries. Many cities could get library service, of a sort, at a cheaper price, but they will lose out on many of the indirect, unmeasured benefits that traditional libraries provide, most important of which is a collection that provides some degree of variety. Librarians in public institutions have a wide degree of freedom in what they can select, even if they often don't choose to exercise that freedom.

On the other hand, the chain libraries will, no doubt, have a warehouse centrally located where they will keep one copy of controversial books, like *Hit Man*, available for loan to any of their local chain operations where it must be requested by each individual patron (signed in triplicate) for a loan period not to exceed three days. Controversial materials will be available — on demand. But the chain library will not go out of its way to make such materials easily available.

The communities that have the most to gain from the advent of the chain library are the smaller communities of about 20,000 or less where, although library service is fairly broad, the collection is pretty much limited to only those items recommended by *Booklist* or *Library Journal*. Small press and scholarly press materials are already pretty scarce, except for a few books that are of local or regional interest. In these small libraries, the occasional copy of *Sensuous Massage for Lovers* that gets sent there by accident from the corporate warehouse will no doubt cause a stir, and perhaps even a local controversy; maybe headquarters would have to send the corporate lawyer to town on the next plane... Not!

Only librarians and eccentric publishers care about censorship enough to resist the impulse to simply play dead when the censor shows up at the door.

For the librarian, the costs/benefits will follow a similar trend. In the larger cities a librarian who finds him or herself suddenly outsourced from a civil service position to a corporate drone position will probably earn less money and have considerably less autonomy in the way he or she does library service. In this sense, librarians will be very much like doctors working for HMOs or corporately-owned hospitals. There will be more rules, but the rules will seem to be a bit more rational, or at least more predictable. Anyone who has worked for a library board, as opposed to a corporate headquarters, can readily see the differences. Instead of playing bridge with the board member once a month, you end up playing golf with the visiting corporate manager twice a year. Both forms of managerial control are a mixture of rational and irrational methods. But with the library board the librarian has more personal autonomy, along with a greater need to be responsive to the peculiar whims of the board.

For the librarian in the smaller community, the act of being outsourced may actually result in better pay and more job security. At the same time, the librarian would be forced to deal with both a library board and a corporate management. A nimble librarian might be able to create a good deal of autonomy by playing the two forces off against each other, but for most people serving two masters usually creates more problems than benefits.

In terms of the collection, the chain librarian in a small community will have less access to materials to select from, but may, as a result, take the collection process more seriously, especially in terms of trying to "milk" materials out of the corporate headquarters. A group of librarians working for the same chain could plan to ask for the same book at the same time, like *The Zinn Reader*, creating a fake "demand" and thus manipulate the system to consider providing all the chain libraries with copies of a particular book. In effect, librarians would be forced to learn how to manipulate the system in order to get certain types of materials into the library collection. This kind of activity is typical where decision-making has been centralized and automated. Workers quickly learn how to manipulate the system and put "spin" on the information sent upstairs to be used by the corporate decision-makers. Many chain libraries in smaller communities may end up with a larger proportion of "liberal" materials, overall, than they had when they were responsive only to requests from the local community.

In terms of the collection, one library will pretty much resemble another, much the same way any one Barnes & Noble store resembles any one Waldenbooks. Actually, a more accurate comparison would be with bookstores that specialize in carrying remaindered titles, since chain libraries will be buying a lot of these to help their "bottom line."

At the same time the book jobbers will use their chain libraries as a place to dump unwanted titles, much like what happened in Hawaii, where dozens of copies of Newt Gingrich's novel *1945* ended up on the shelves. Most of these chain libraries can expect to serve as a white elephants' graveyard for remaindered titles, damaged copies, etc., as the book jobbers learn to exploit them to benefit their own bottom lines. All in all, chain libraries will do for your community what corporate hog farming did for Iowa, except in this case the effluvia doesn't run into the river, it becomes a part of your collection.

In terms of gifts, the chain librarian may be more or less open to accepting gift books and gift subscriptions, depending on the policies of the corporation. But again, there is certain to be a loss of autonomy when it comes to adding gifts, especially since the chain library will have to consider the dollar costs of cataloging when considering whether or not to add "marginal" materials. Chain libraries will also almost certainly put into place a variety of user fees for interlibrary loans, computer searches, etc. Patrons should expect to take up the slack as the library concentrates on padding the "bottom line." At the same time, these libraries are likely to encourage the use of "free" material on the internet in place of costly books and periodicals, and they will tend to encourage use of sources of free or relatively cheap information that may be questionable in terms of accuracy and currency. Access to more expensive information may be limited to patrons willing to pay a little extra.

In the future, chain libraries are also likely to be targeted by marketing specialists as a place where there is a captive audience for advertising. In the future, the main concern will not be with filters that block access to pornography. Rather, installing "commercial" filters will be a standard procedure for the chain library. These filters will channel patrons toward certain targeted products and corporate sites that have paid the chain library for access to the patrons. These same filters, in addition to blocking "pornography" on the net, could be used to block access to websites for labor unions, environmental causes, and other "radical" enterprises. In other words, the library is likely to remain an agent for conventional "liberal" social forces, and the chain library is likely to continue and even advance this role, especially as a change agent in small towns.

Unfortunately, as with the rapidly increasing spread of corporate-controlled medicine through HMOs, etc., the emergence of the chain library is likely to begin in large cities where there is a lot of money to be made, rather than by targeting small town libraries, which would be only marginally profitable. So, at least in the short run, the chain library is likely to harm librarianship as a profession. Most librarians should start memorizing the lines "Do you want paper or plastic bags for your books?" and "Do you want fries with that pay-per-view internet search?"

> Toxteth riots, England, 1981. During a lull in the action a leftist militant climbs on to a box and addresses the crowd on the subject of the coming socialist utopia. Her promise that there will be jobs for all is met with derisory laughter from a group of young rioters. As the speaker details other reforms, the group begins a mocking chant, 'Bigger cages, longer chains! "Bigger cages, longer chains!"— Larry Law.

REFERENCES

Coffman, Steve. "What If You Ran Your Library Like a Bookstore?" *American Libraries* 29:3 (March 1998): 40-46.

Intner, Sheila. "The Good Professional: A New Vision." *American Libraries* 29:3 (March 1998): 48-50.

Law, Larry. *Bigger Cages, Longer Chains*. London: Dark Star Press, 1991.

Chapter 11

The Ongoing Corruption of the Arts

There is an ongoing corruption of our profession, moving as it is away from librarianship as a vocation within the liberal arts and toward librarianship as a branch of "information management"—a fairly new field of study that has its origins in figuring out the cheapest way to write a telegram. In a very real sense information management is more closely related to various types of data handling, even direct-mail marketing, than to traditional librarianship. In the worldview of the information manager, the fundamental goal for librarians is finding out how we can use technology, and particularly automation, to improve library service. A close examination of the quality of that information is not needed, or even wanted. What is wanted is information, even fairly useless information, provided in a cheap (or not so cheap) and timely manner, much the same way that the daily newspaper provides stock quotes, irrespective of whether the price of a stock on any given day bears any real relationship to the actual performance of the corporation or the value of its stock.

Similarly, many librarians feel that it is their duty to provide the latest novels, movie videos and music recordings, regardless of whether these have any value beyond the current fad. The sheer fact of a media-generated "demand" is sufficient reason for buying this stuff. For example, I wonder how many libraries wasted $23 on Andrei Codrescu's novel *Blood Countess*, based on Codrescu's popularity as a news commentator? And how many libraries waste money on movie tie-in books? Most librarians should not be faulted for wanting to at least try to meet this so-called "popular" demand. The failure is when we don't go beyond this and provide substantial material in the arts for our patrons, rather than just the latest bestsellers. This should be considered another argument for recruiting librarians from the liberal arts, rather than business or computer science.

During a recent visit to the local post office, I found the clerk, who was working behind the counter, crooning a popular tune, mainly out-of-key and in a voice that would make a frog wince. After he noticed me standing at the counter, he apologized, "If I had any voice at all, I'd have gone into music!" Trying to be helpful, I responded, "Well, there's still country music." He responded with a look that suggested he had meant the honorable vocation of country music all along.

Similarly, I've tried to understand the current vogue of New Age music, which usually combines "nature" sounds with a synthesizer in order to aim toward the high art of the elevator. Recently, I tried listening to a recording of "The Delta," which included birds, a frog, several hundred bugs, and an electronic synthesizer. I honestly tried to "visualize" the scene, but I kept wondering where the heck they were able to plug in the synthesizer and how they were able to keep the mosquitoes away from the musician. And then I kept seeing, in my mind's eye, the Budweiser frog sitting on a log. And, after awhile, I started wishing I had a rock that I could throw at that frog so I could get him to shut the hell up. This musical number was followed by a recording of "The Arctic," which was mainly wind sounds, punctuated with the howling of wolves and the electronic sounds of the synthesizer. I tried visualizing again, and imagined a musician — who looked something like Yanni — playing the synthesizer out on a frozen lake. But I couldn't figure out what to do with the wolves howling in the background. And then I imagined the wolves chewing on Yanni's legs while he played soulfully on the synthesizer. So much for my appreciation of the New Age.

The only music I can think of that is more vacuous than New Age music is the stuff called "Christian rock." Now there's an oxymoron if I ever heard one. I don't think anyone questions the fact that Christian rock is strictly derivative, a pale shadow of rock 'n' roll. As much as these musicians may try to imitate the good stuff, it just doesn't come off very well. But I'm waiting for a Christian version of "Hotel California" before I definitely make up my mind about Christian rock. Usually with Christian rock, we end up with music that sounds vaguely like 70s classical rock ballads or, worse yet, love songs that interject Christ into the tune in the role of the lover. The result of these efforts is usually some strange hybrid that doesn't make sense, and doesn't even sound good. Few Christian rock groups manage to struggle up out of mediocrity, though when they do, as with DC Talk's *Jesus Freak* album, they do manage to come up with one or two good sounds.

It's not that I am so enamored of rock 'n' roll that I would defend it from its genuine critics. Rather, I believe that creative artists should be given credit for originality and inventiveness, and that artists who are imitative and derivative should be recognized for their lack of ability rather than being praised (even if it is only praise in the religious media) and lionized as creative geniuses. When someone like C.S. Lewis is held up for excessive praise, I feel that a disservice is being done to the really creative people whom C.S. Lewis imitated. In what way was Lewis innovative in his Perelandra series? What did he do that hadn't already been done by Edgar Rice Burroughs or H.G. Wells? Furthermore, there are serious problems with what Lewis tried to teach through his fiction. It would take too long to cover this topic here, but readers can look to David Holbrook's *The Skeleton in the Wardrobe* for a complete analysis of the serious problems with Lewis's work.

There is no question in my mind that Mark Twain was a better writer than C.S. Lewis, and I doubt that this belief has anything to do with my agreement with Twain's views and disagreement with Lewis's. Anyone who has seen the film biography of Lewis, called *Shadowlands*, should understand what I'm talking about here. Lewis was seriously impaired in the area of his humanity, like a deadly wound of the spirit. His life is the stuff of morbid mental disease, and it should not be encouraged in the young, who ought to be emulating Ozzy Osbourne instead. I, for one, would rather see my children getting high and biting the heads off bats than morbidly brooding over some theological issue while practicing self-flagellation in a Cambridge watercloset.

In the case of C.S. Lewis, we can see that people who wish to see the Christian faith as "respectable" may be searching for a role model. I once, many years ago, had a great deal of respect for C.S. Lewis, a respect that I now realize was largely misplaced. My wife, on the other hand, was rather fond of Teilhard de Chardin during her misspent youth in the ladies lounge of St. Norbert College. Both Lewis and Teilhard de Chardin were accomplished apologists for their respective belief systems. And Teilhard de Chardin, in particular, is widely read by Christians who are at the point of leaving the faith and need an extra little push. Both these philosophers have a certain appeal, especially to young adults at transitional stages in their intellectual growth and maturation. But most religious philosophy, like religious art, is limited intellectually and never rises above being imitative and banal. This is especially true for "popular" religious art, like Christian rock music.

The problem for Christian rock music is, of course, that very little of contemporary rock music can be "converted" to their uses. For example, I can imagine a Christian rendition of "Purple Rain" but the music video would probably have a bit too much gore to be shown on MTV. Not that the goriness of the video would inhibit the purveyors of Christian rock. Most Christian fundamentalists have a fairly large blind spot when it comes to the bad taste of their own self-glorifying art. For example, I'm sure millions of people have seen the television advertisement where Christ takes the place of a death row criminal in the electric chair. Even more bizarre is a recent flurry of Christian T-shirts emphasizing blood and torture, in bold exciting colors, along with lurid quotations about the "sacrifice" of Christ and blunt threats of punishment and eternal damnation to those souls so foolish as to reject His infinite love and forgiveness. I myself own a "Lord's Gym" T-shirt that shows Christ doing push-ups with a huge wooden cross on his back. The cross is labeled "The Sins of the World" and across the bottom it is has the motto: "Bench Press This!" The back of the shirt has a hand, pierced with a spike, and plenty of flowing blood, along with the motto "His Pain, Your Gain." On the other hand, maybe bad taste comes quite naturally to some people, along with a fondness for whips, thorns, nails, the smell of boot leather and the taste for blood.

For example, Gerald L.K. Smith, the founder of The Christ of the Ozarks resort in Eureka Springs, Arkansas, has to be the winner and grand champion of all time in bad taste. Not only is his gigantic concrete statue of Christ, called "The Christ of the Ozarks," one of the ugliest statues ever created, he has a collection of religious art in his "Christ-Only" gallery that apparently has to be seen to be believed. Friends tell me that it includes group portraits of Smith and his wife with Christ (if only he would include Elvis and do it on black velvet — now that would be something!). This collection of "art" combined with the ugly statue and his horrendously long and boring "Passion Play"— performed in a so-called reconstruction of the Holy Land — well, the mind boggles that one man in one lifetime could be responsible for so much ugliness! Gerald L.K. Smith, who died a few years ago, was the purveyor of all sorts of ugliness. In addition to his lousy art, he proclaimed himself "America's best known anti–Semite" and published a series of hate-filled publications over many decades. It's probably true that visual ugliness, at least in the arts, reveals and explores an inward ugliness that might otherwise remain hidden.

Unfortunately, we are now in the middle of a popular revival of other Fundamentalist Christian art forms, including Christian novels, and even Christian fantasy and science fiction. In my opinion, Christian literature died with Dostoyevsky. And, to paraphrase Senator Lloyd Bentsen, "I read Dostoyevsky; I liked Dostoyevsky. But these new writers are no Dostoyevsky." Most of Christian literature, including the work of C.S. Lewis, is derivative and shallow, imitating much better work by sincere artists. Unfortunately, there is little left in the world today called "Christian" that isn't derivative and imitative of someone else — usually an artist with real emotions, real ideas, and (most importantly) real talent.

This is not a criticism of Christianity so much as a recognition that there is a lot of mediocrity, self-indulgence and selfishness in the world which wraps itself up in the garments of religion, or patriotism, or art — and sometimes, as with Gerald L.K. Smith, all three at the same time. The mix of patriotism with religion is a potent combination, as anyone who has enjoyed *The 700 Club* on television can tell you. Contemporary evangelical Christian culture is like a Frankenstein's monster, made up of all sorts of strange parts and possessing the power to go on, and on, and on — in spite of what common sense would seem to tell us about the viability of such a creature. Amazingly, this culture is alive and well, and it produces thousands of new book titles a year, not to mention the various serial publications.

The library must, of course, try to be inclusive in its selection policies. And that means buying representative selections of this dreadful muck for the collection. To some extent, librarians can rely on the generosity of individual churches and church members in collecting these materials. And since much of it is repetitive, the librarian can concentrate on collecting reference materials and books by major figures while relying mainly on gifts to fill any other gaps in the collection. The librarian can sleep peacefully at night, knowing that the progress of civilization will not be harmed by the lack of these materials in the collection.

References

Codrescu, Andrei. *The Blood Countess: A Novel*. New York: Simon & Schuster, 1995.

Dc Talk. *Jesus Freak* (album). Nashville: Mix Music, 1995.

Jeansonne, Glen. *Gerald L.K. Smith: Minister of Hate*. New Haven: Yale, 1988.

Chapter 12

Conclusion: Censorship into the Millennium

Late in the 1930s the Kansas City area was suffering under a terrible drought. A group of local pastors decided to hold a prayer meeting in the football stadium and pray for rain. As the ministers began to gather, a Unitarian minister, well-known for his sense of irony, showed up at the stadium carrying his umbrella. When people asked why he was carrying the umbrella, he quipped, "I'm carrying it because I believe in the power of prayer!" Needless to say, he was the only member of the religious meeting who was carrying an umbrella that day. And, in spite of the many prayers offered that day, the drought continued for several months.

Most librarians function a bit like that minister. We keep hoping for the best while preparing for the worst. And with censorship issues, the arrival of the censor is a mixed blessing. The problem is that, in spite of having a federal government established on the (almost) firm commitment to protect people's rights, there is a constant drumbeat from political extremists to censor, and through censorship to control. For librarians this means a constant effort to educate and re-educate the public on censorship issues.

As times change, the methods of the censor change. Today the most serious challenge is that posed by "fiscal" censorship. By that, I mean that censors are finding it quite easy to generate support for creating legal mandates that prohibit spending state moneys on "controversial" materials based on their subject content. Recently, a representative of the state legislature of Kansas asked the six state universities to provide information on how many courses were being taught that deal with homosexuality and bisexuality. The universities, and their faculty, quickly surmised that the only reason for asking such a question would be if you were planning to restrict or control the content of the courses through legislation. This request followed, by only a few days, the passage in the legislature of restrictions on the state's medical university, prohibiting the teaching of surgical abortion techniques to interns.

These events are evidence for two of the most promising lines of attack for the censor. First, the political Right has discovered that the abortion issue has pretty much petered out as a way of rallying the troops. So the right-wingers have turned to attacks on "deviant" sexual behavior as a way to inspire the troops for a new crusade. This is clearly shown by Operation Rescue's decision to picket Disney World during "Gay Day," an annual weekend-long party that attracts gays and lesbians from all over the country. In addition, Operation Rescue plans to picket Night of Joy, a popular Christian music event held at Disney World and attended by young Christians who, obviously, ignore the Christian right and its ongoing boycott of Disney.

Second, right-wing politicians have figured out that, although most people will agree with the principles of free speech and a free press, many of them will support fiscal censorship. This trend is in line with the history of the abortion movement, as it was the effort by states to provide poor women with free abortions that led to a violent reaction from the Right, and the rapid growth of the Right-to-Life movement. Their first step was to prohibit spending tax dollars on abortions, but today this same prohibition is easily applied to using tax dollars to teach medical students how to perform abortions or to using tax dollars to teach about family planning in general.

Just this year the children's librarian in the Mexico-Audrain County (Missouri) Library was fired, at the instigation of the local Family Friendly Libraries group. The group had demanded that the library remove all materials relating to "sensitive family issues" including "sexuality, the death of a loved one, or the birth process." Since the library is publicly funded, right-wing organizations feel that it is perfectly proper for them to engage in censorship of the materials in the library. And this type of argument is being used more and more frequently.

Similarly, Senator McCain has introduced legislation at the federal level that would force libraries to install filters on all their computers that access the internet, or risk losing their special E-Rate. It is not by coincidence that these internet filters, used to block access to "pornography," also typically block access to sites that have information relating to abortion and "deviant" sexuality, and a whole range of issues relating to minorities, family planning, etc.

Our best defense against these efforts by the Right to roll back hard-won victories is to take back our profession. This means reclaiming the American Library Association, supporting liberal projects and organizations, like the Progressive Librarians Guild, and beginning a defense of our profession as a profession. This last step is the most vital because, if we are reduced to being little more than Wal-Mart–style greeters, there is no way as a profession that we can hope to muster the kind of political and economic force needed to support and maintain the basic civil rights of the middle class, let along participate in expanding those civil rights to include the underclass. Expanding our base of support to include the lower classes is necessary if we are to survive as a profession into the next century. This means making common cause with other liberal institutions and organizations on a whole range of issues, from defending free speech to supporting the minimum wage. After all, some day we may need the protection of the minimum wage laws ourselves.

Index